EVOLUTION OF THE
PEDAL CAR

VOL. 2

Edited by Neil S. Wood

Copyright 1990

L-W BOOK SALES
P.O. Box 69
Gas City, IN 46933

ISBN# 0-89145-444-6

TABLE OF CONTENTS

Introduction

   Children's Pedal Car interest has grown in the past few years to an almost unbelievable proportion. It is one of the most desirable, fastest appreciating collectibles to be found today. It is now an adult toy.

   There were five well known early manufacturers of pedal cars; American National, Gendron, Steelcraft, Garton and Toledo Wheel. These companies are all out of business today. Deluxe pedal cars were only bought by the wealthy in the 1920s and 1930s making it very difficult to find one in really good condition. Some full size car collectors are selling their collections and going into pedal car collecting since there is no maintenance to pedal cars.

   Pedal cars of the 1920s and 1930s are a big part of American history. They have moved from the sidewalks into the living rooms for decorating, displays, etc. They are nice to admire under the Christmas tree for decoration instead of gifts for children. Good luck in your pedaling !

Pricing

   The price guide in this book is for Pedal Cars in good to excellent condition. Cars found with parts missing, very poor paint, wheels changed from originals, or excessive rust will bring much lower prices. A car considered to be in good condition is one with original paint and no parts missing. A car in excellent condition is one that is 70% to 95% mint. This price guide is based on cars in these conditions. L-W books can not be responsible for gains or losses, as this is ONLY A GUIDE.

A very special thanks to the following people for without their help this publication would not have been possible:

Darwin Hunkler, Marvin Bishop (our layout man), Nathan Clement (our printer), Gary Wood (press operator), Steve Wickham (layout man) and a special thanks to Elmer Duellman and Randall Arteburn. I bothered Elmer and Randall both night and day and would have been lost without their advice.

So to all

Thanks

We would also like to thank everyone who sent us pictures and information. If we could not use your picture because of quality or other reason we are truly sorry. We also had some problems reading some addresses and names and hope that we came up with the correct information. If we did make a mistake on your pedal car information please accept our aploogy.

Elmer Duellman is an advanced collector. As usual he is always interested in buying, selling and trading to upgrade his fine collection. You may contact him at:

Rt. 2, Box 26
Fountain City, WI 54629

Elmer Duellman wants to buy a 1958 Chevy Pedal Car plastic body by Hamilton

Phone 608-687-9211

I

COLLECTORS & CONTRIBUTORS

Albert, Ray - 170A Spahr-Seiling Rd. #2 - Dillsburg, PA 17019
Arterburn, Randall - 21 So. Addison - Indianapolis, IN 46222
Aust, Ronald - 3715 Volquardsen Ave. - Davenport, IA 52806
Barker, Rex - P. O. Box 949 - Lasalle, CO 80645
Barry, David - P. O. Box 46 - Epping, NSW 2121, Australia
Block, Todd - 603 Invenness Ln. - St. Peter, MN 56082
Buchanan, John - 671 S. Water - Marine City, MI 48039
Burt, Gene - RD 1, Box 302 - Pleasantville, PA 16341
Buske, Earl R. - P. O. Box 129 - Pocohontas, IA 50574
Cain, E. G. - 8603 Butler-Warren - West Chester, OH 45069
Chaussee, Calvin - 1530 Kenland Ct. - Colorado Springs, CO 80915
Clemens, Rick - 24481 S. Larkin Rd. - Beavercreek, OR 97004
Depenbrok, Bob - 9665 Venna Ave. - Arleta, CA 91331
Dodd, Richard - 629 S. Scenic - Springfield, MO 65802
Domanik, Joe - 6501 River Meadows Turn - Racine, WI 53402
Duellman, Elmer - Rt. 2, Box 26 - Fountain City, WI 54629
Ellsworth, Bob - 1207 Charter Oak Dr. - Taylors, SC 29687
Elwell, Mike - 7412 Iden Ave. So. - Cottage Grove, MN 55016
Endres, Terry - P. O. Box 22 - Fort Collins, CO 80522
Fisher, Danny - 1921 Castle Dr. - Garland, TX 75040
Funkhouser, Ron - Rt. 1, Box 496 - Tomsbrook, VA 22660
Giolma, Clive - 700 Downie St. - Kamloops, BC, Can. V2B 5T2
Guggemos, Bill - 1104 N. Creyts Rd. - Lansing, MI 48917
Hauschka, Kurt - 116 Chamberlain St. - Rochester, NH 03867
Hughes, Blake - 6848 Donahoo - Kansas City, KS 66104
Hunkler, Darwin - RR 2, Box 198 - Russiaville, IN 46901
Juenemann, Roy - 6024 Sullivan - Wichita, KS 67204
Keehn, Charles - 540 Kinderkamack Rd. - River Edge, NJ 07661
Kellar, Bob - 61 Macon St. - Sayville, NY 11782
Kirk, Joe - 551 Central Ave. - Shafter, CA 93263
Kirsch, Gene - 2074 Western Ave. No. - Roseville, MN 55113
Koch, Michael - 495 Dallas Dr. - Thousand Oaks, CA 91360
Kyber, Robert - 14 Lake Rd. - Chatham Township, NJ 07928
Laduca, David - 5138 Daha Dr. - Lewiston, NY 14092
Linkous, Blaine - P. O. Box 178 - Fallston, MD 21047
Lynch, Bill - 2330 Elm - Bellingham, WA 98225
McKenzie - P. O. Box 111 - Seal Beach, CA 90740
Parker, Chas - RD 2, Box 368 - Tarentum, PA 15084
Parkhurst, Jim - 256 South Ave. - Bridgeton, NJ 08302
Phillips, Stan - 438 8th St. - Oakmont, PA 15139
Powers, Steve - 119 Arden Dr. - So. San Francisco, CA 94080
Reed, David - P. O. Box 653 - Redding, CT 06896
Richter, Dave - 6817 Sutherland - Mentor, OH 44060
Ricker's Antiques - RD 1 - Mill Hall, PA 17751
Robidoux, Kurt - 1234 S. 9th St. - Lincoln, NE 68502
Roy, Aaron - 817 Edgehill - Ashland, OH 44805
Sandhill Antiques - 1000 W. Main St. - Robins, IA 52328
Sawyer, Dwight - Chatham Auto Body - Chatham, NY
Schneider, Larry - 9476 S. 27th St. - Oak Dreek, WI 53154
Spadone, Dennis - 10 Rose Ct. - Denville, NJ 07834
Stack, Art - 2990 Transit Rd. - Buffalo, NY 14224
Steele, Ross - Rt. 5, Box 005588 - Madisonville, TN 37354
Torel, M. J. - 1620 Palmcroft Dr. SW - Phoenix, AZ 85007
Turk, Jerry - 4240 Carvel Ln. - Edgewater, MD 21037

Vidaurri, Darrell - 17547 Fernwood Dr. - Jamestown, CA 95327
Wattawa, Don - 3578 W. Parnell Ave. - Milwaukee, WI 53221
Wickfelder, Jim - 16934 Cicero - Tinley Park, IL 60477

CONTRIBUTING DEALERS & RESTORERS

Applegate, Dean - 6531 Downs Rd. - Warren, OH 44481
Arterburn, Randall - 21 So. Addison - Indianapolis, IN 46222
Barker, Rex - P. O. Box 949 - Lasalle, CO 80645
Branch, Charles - Rt. 8, Box 524 - Marshall, TX 75670
Depenbrok, Bob - 9665 Vena Ave. - Arleta, CA 91331
Dodd, Richard - 629 S. Scenic - Springfield, MO 65802
Duellman, Elmer - Rt. 2, Box 26 - Fountain City, WI 54629
Ellsworth, Bob - 1207 Charter Oak Dr. - Taylors, SC 29687
Geary, Jim - Rt. 14, Box 125 - Goldsboro, NC 27530
Gordon, Frank - 9622 Lee Blvd. - Leawood, KS 66206
Hemmelman, Harold - RR 1 - Centerville, WI 54630
Holder, Kerry - Rt. 20, Box 245 - Springfield, MO 65803
Hunkler, Darwin - RR 2, Box 198 - Russiaville, IN 46901
Hurd, James L. - 217 No. Jefferson St. - Chicago, IL 60606
King, Dick - 1811 Baker Way Loop - Kelso, WA 98626
Knox, Donald - 1941 Vinland Rd. - Oshkosh, WI 54901
Lampman, Robert - RD #1, Box 73-0 - Vernon, NY 13476
Nestle, Paul - P. O. Box 59 - Nipomo, CA 93444
Olimpio, Marc - P. O. Box 1505 - Wolfeboro, NH 03894
Portell Restorations - 1574 Saddle Dr. - Festus, MO 63028
Premer, Paul - P. O. Box 103 - Evans, CO 80620
Sandhill Antiques - 1000 West Main St. - Robins, IA 52328
Sawyer, Dwight - Chatham Auto Body - Chatham, NY
Torr, William - 527 White Ave. - Northvale, NJ 07647
Weirick, Ed - RFD #3, Box 190 - Ellsworth, ME 04605
Wilson, Allen - 1709 Santa Cecilia - Kingsville, TX 78363

K

Places To Go - Reading To Do

Following are shows you don't want to miss if you are interested in Pedal Cars and other toys and related items.

L-W Toy Show, Indiana State Fairgrounds, Indianapolis, December
Info: L-W Promotions, P. O. Box 69, Gas City, IN 46933
Phone 317-674-6450

Dayton, Ohio M.C.T.A. Show, April & October
Info: M.C.T.A., P.O. Box 403 N.D. Station, Dayton, OH 45404
Phone 513-233-8381

Antique Toy & Doll World, St. Charles, IL, April, June, October
Info: Antique World Shows, Inc., P.O. Box 34509, Chicago, IL 60634
Phone 312-725-0633

NATIONAL ANTIQUE ADVERTISING SHOW, Indiana St. Frgrnds, Indianapolis
March, June, October
Info: L-W Promotions, P. O. Box 69, Gas City, IN 46933
Phone 317-674-6450   Neil

Brimfield, Mass. Shows in May, July, and September
Phone 413-245-3436

Greenville, SC Pedal Car & Toy Show, Memorial Weekend
Phone 803-244-4308

COLLECTORS CARNIVAL, Indiana State Fairgrounds, Indianapolis
March & October
Phone 317-674-6450   Scott

Hershey, Pennsylvania, National AACA Meet, October

Kalamazoo, MI, Antique Toy Circus Maximus
3rd Saturday in May, Saturday after Thanksgiving
Info: 1720 Rupert, Grand Rapids, MI 49505
Phone 616-361-9887

If you deal in Pedal Cars or related items, the following publications will will be of interest to you.

Collectors Showcase, P. O. Box 837, Tulsa, OK 74101
Wheel Goods Trader, P. O. Box 435, Fraser, MI 48026
Antique Trader, P. O. Box 1050, Dubuque, IA 52001
Antique Toy World, P. O. Box 34509, Chicago, IL 60634
U. S. Toy Collector, P. O. Box 4244, Missoula, MT 59806

The Book on Pedal Cars!

8½" x 11" Softbound – 240 Pages 27 pages in full color

$29.⁹⁵ *Price Guide Included*

Send $29.95 plus
$2.00 shipping to:
L-W Book Sales
Box 69
Gas City, IN 46933

**C.O.D.
Mastercard & Visa
Orders Only
1-800-777-6450**
All Other Inquiries
1-317-674-6450

Dealer Inquiries Invited

**This is the one and
only book you will
need on Pedal Cars.**

**EVOLUTION OF THE
PEDAL CAR
and Other Riding Toys
with prices
1884 – 1970's**

Pedal Cars – Sleds – Scooters – Tricycles – and More

*100's of Pedal Cars
and Riding Toys
Pictured*

Don't Miss Out!

**170 Actual Catalog pages from 1884 thru the 1970's. Black and white pictures of cars
and toys, postcards and original (old) pictures of kids in cars. Over 27 pages of restored cars and toys, in full living color. Most cars are priced. Many auction prices
and private sale prices of individual cars plus price averages on others.**

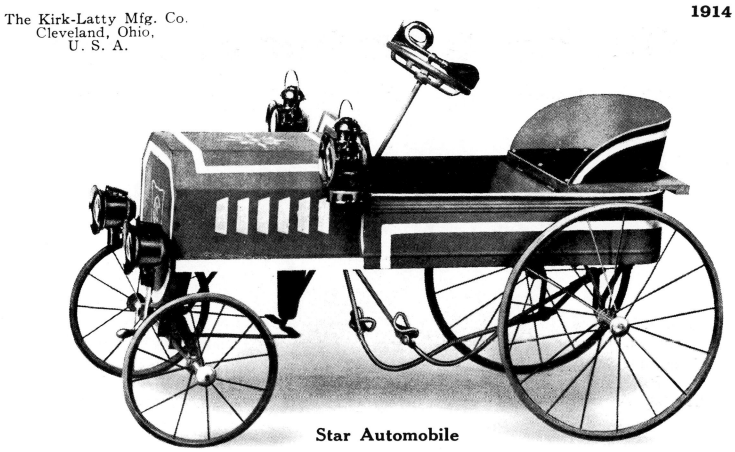

Star Automobile

Beauty Automobile

The Kirk-Latty Mfg. Co.
Cleveland, Ohio,
U. S. A.

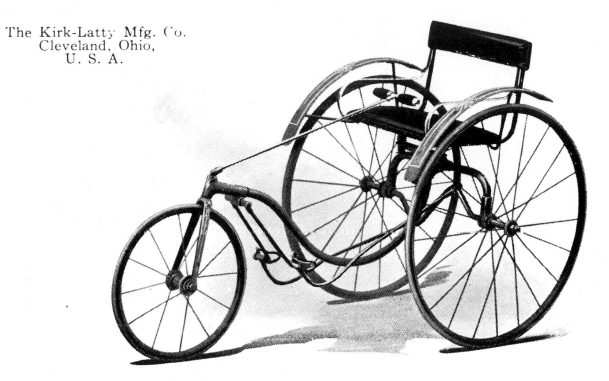

Cleveland Queen High Grade Ball Bearing Tricycle

Gem Hand Car

The Kirk-Latty Mfg. Co.
Cleveland, Ohio,
U. S. A.

1914

Fore Door Automobile

Lakewood Automobile

Cadillac Automobile

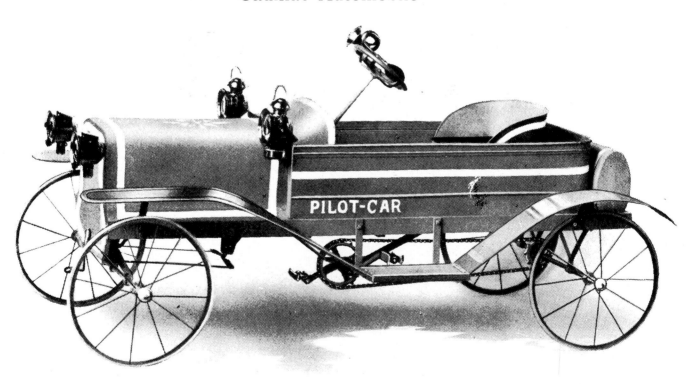

Pilot Car Automobile

THE "WINTON."

No. 380. **Body** 14x31 in. **Wheels** 8 and 14 in., with ⅜ in. Rubber Tires.

Body of hardwood and sheet steel, finished in green and red, with gold and yellow stenciling and striping.

Wheels and **running gear** finished in black baked enamel.

THE "BUICK."

No. 382. Body 15½x37 in. **Wheels** 10 and 16 in., with ½ in. Rubber Tires.

Body of hardwood, with heavy sheet steel hood, finished in ombination of blue, green and yellow, with gold stencil and striping.

Wheels and **running gear** finished in black baked enamel.

Seat upholstered in leatherette.

Ratchet starting crank.

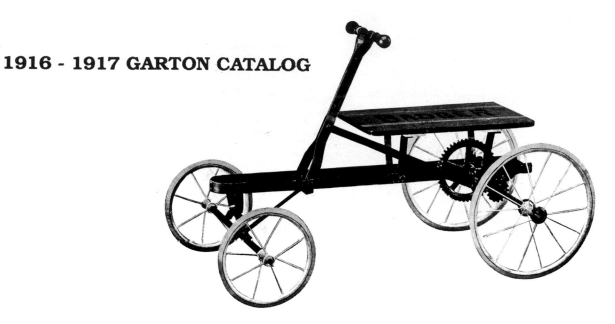

"BADGER" HAND CAR.

No. 501. Junior Size.

Steel frame enameled back.

Driving gear so constructed as to permit of no dead center.

Wheels black enamel with ½ in. rubber tires.

Black enamel handle grips with brass ferrules.

Wheels 8 and 10 in. Seat 7x12 in.

THE "BARNEY OLDFIELD RACER."

Bodies made of hardwood and sheet steel, finished in combination blue and red, stenciled and striped in black and gold.

Seats upholstered in leatherette.

Ratchet starting crank.

Gear and **wheels** finished in black baked enamel.

No. 385. Body 13x43 in. **Wheels** 12 in., with ⅜ in. Rubber Tires. 6 in. wood rim steering wheel. Gasoline tank on rear. Shipping weight 50 lbs. each.

No. 386. Body 13x43 in. **Barrel Hub Wheels** 12 in., with ⅝ in. Rubber Tires. 6 in. wood rim steering wheel. Gasoline tank and 2 extra tires on rear. Seat upholstered in leatherette.

THE "PACKARD."

Bodies made of hard wood and sheet steel, finished red, green, blue or gray, striped and stenciled in gold.

Wheels and **running gear** finished in black baked enamel.

Seat is adjustable.

No. 371.   **Body** 15x26 in.   **Wheels** 10 and 16 in., with ½ in. Rubber Tires.

1916 - 1917 GARTON CATALOG

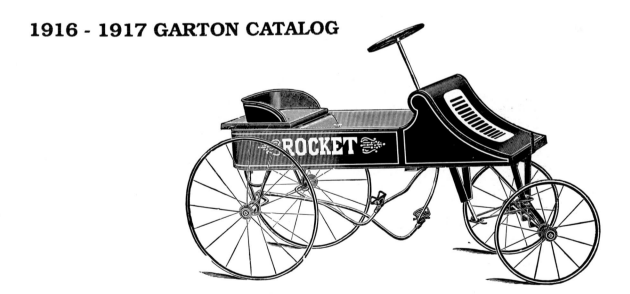

THE "HUMMER."

Bodies of sheet steel and hard wood, finished in red, striped and stenciled in gold and green.

Wheels and running gear finished in black baked enamel.

No. 374.   **Body** 14x30 in.   **Wheels** 10 and 16 in., Steel Tires.

THE "PEERLESS."

No. 372. **Body** 15x36 in. **Wheels** 10 and 16 in., with ⅝ in. Rubber Tires.

Body of sheet steel and hard wood, finished in Battleship Gray, beautifully striped and stenciled.

Seat upholstered in leatherette.

1916 - 1917 GARTON CATALOG

Tractor

Model No. B690

(For Children 4 to 7 Years)

SPECIFICATIONS

OVERALL DIMENSIONS: Length 43″; height 26″.

WHEELS: Beaded rear 16″ diameter with 1¼″ solid rubber tires. Beaded front 8″ dia.. with ¾″ solid rubber tires. Equipped with new plated hub caps.

EQUIPMENT: Adjustable rubber pedals, spring saddle, draw bar.

FINISH: Body in Green baked enamel with Ivory trim. Seat and seat spring in Black. Wheels in Ivory.

THE "PIERCE ARROW."

No. 370.   **Body** 14x30 in., made of sheet steel and hardwood, painted red or green, striped and stenciled. Equipped with ratchet starting crank.

Wheels 10 and 14 in., finished in baked black enamel, with ⅜ in. rubber tires.

Gear wrought iron finished in baked black enamel.

1916 - 1917 GARTON CATALOG

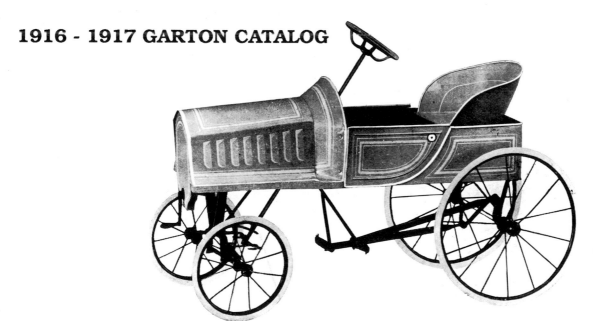

THE "POPE."

No. 378.   **Body** 13x36 in.   **Wheels** 10 and 16 in., with ½ in. tires.

Body of heavy sheet steel and hard wood, finished in blue, gray or yellow, with striping and stenciling in gold and other colors to harmonize with body.

Hinged seat forming tool box in rear.

Ratchet starting crank.

Wheels and **running gear** finished in black baked enamel.

KEYSTONE STEEL "RIDE 'EM" TOYS

With Electric Headlights (Less Batteries)

No. 6400—Locomotive. Automatic whistle and moving pistons. Searchlight, two green electric lights. Adjustable handle bar. Eight solid rubber wheels. Brass trimmings. Couplings can connect locomotive with freight or pullman car. Length, 28 inches. Shipping weight, 18½ lbs. Each...........**$6.25**

No. 6100—Locomotive. Red boiler and cradle, ivory cab. Rubber tired wheels 3⅜ inches in diameter. Electric searchlight. Child can steer while sitting on cab. Size, 24¼ inches long. Weight, 10 lbs. 3 oz. Each...........**$2.50**

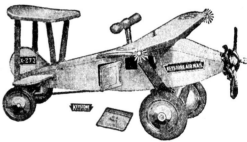

No. 6800 — Pullman Car. Two electric lights on inside. Handle bar for steering control. Can be coupled to locomotive. Top lifts up—lots of room inside for toys. Length, 25 inches. Shipping weight, 17¾ lbs. Each...........**$5.00**

No. 56—Water Tower. Two electric lights, spotlight and siren horn. Hand operated pressure pump. Handle bar for steering. Removable seat. Water tank. Ladders. Brass railings. Aluminum running boards. Bell. Length, 29 inches. Shipping weight, 22½ lbs. Each, **$9.50**

WILL SHOOT WATER 30 FEET HIGH

No. 273 — Mail Plane. One green, one red electric light under wing. Plane will not tip. Adjustable handle bar. Four solid rubber tires. Makes clicking noise when pulled. Revolving propeller. Length, 25 inches; height, 24 inches. Shipping weight, 12¼ lbs. Each...........**$3.75**

No. 60—Steam Roller. Extra heavy roller, well proportioned wheels. Loud brass bell. Will carry a weight of about 150 lbs. Each, **$3.00**

No. 47—Steam Shovel (no lights). With handle bar for steering control. When scoop is raised the arm can be extended an additional 8½ inches. A trap door on the scoop automatically locks when the scoop drops to its original position. Housing turns round on turntable. Equipped with automatic ratchet stop, springs, etc. Length, 35½ inches, when arm is extended. Shipping weight, 11 lbs. Each...........**$3.00**

No. 46—Steam Shovel. With similar construction as No. 47 Steam Shovel, without the extension arm feature and without boiler house and coal box. Shipping weight, 9 lbs. Each.......**$1.50**

KEYSTONE STEEL "RIDE 'EM" TOYS

with Electric Headlights (Less Batteries)

No. 79—Aerial Ladder. Electric headlights and spotlight with electric horn operated by push button and connected for batteries. Extra ladders. Handle bar for steering. Removable seat. Aluminum covered running board. 30½ inches long. Ladder fully extended, 51 inches. One in a carton. Weight, 21 lbs.

Each.................................. **$8.50**

No. 49 — Fire Truck. With two headlights and spotlight with adjustable handle bar and removable seat. Extension ladders, hose reel with 12 feet of non-curling hose cord, brass screw nozzle, swinging bell on the radiator. Siren noise maker, cricket type. Brass railings. Length, 27½ inches; height, 10¾ inches; shipping weight, 17 lbs. Each........ **$5.00**

No. 55— Koaster Truck. With two electric headlights. A comfortable coaster for small children. Has adjustable handle bar for steering. Platform of especially heavy material and baked. Shipping weight, 15 lbs.

Each.................................. **$4.00**

No. 38 — Dump Truck. Will hold 250 lbs. Lifting lever on side. Disc wheels, rubber tires. Ribbed body, removable seat. Size, 26 x 10½ inches. One in carton. Weight, 14½ lbs. Each.. **$4.00**

No. 928—Ride 'Em Dump Truck. Green cab and chassis, red pan, green seat. Rubber-tired wheels, 3⅜ inches wide, with painted discs. Two electric headlights and spotlight. Size, 23¼ inches long, 6⅞ inches wide, 9½ inches high. Shipping weight, 8¾ lbs.

Each.................................. **$2.50**

No. 936 — Fire Tower. Red body, solid rubber wheels, 3 inches diameter. Two electric headlights, spotlight, tank and pump arrangement, rubber hose with brass nozzle. Shoots water about 20 feet by working pump. Size, 21¼ inches long, 6½ inches wide, 26 inches high. Shipping weight, 8 lbs.

Each.................................. **$3.35**

NO. 61RBD

Body   Length overall 45 inches. Wheelbase 32 inches. Easy riding springs on rear.

Finish   Royal blue, striped and decorated in yellow and black. Fenders black. Wheels red with green center and green stripes.

Equipment   Auto type molded rubber steering wheel with gas control lever. Horn. Instrument board. Motometer with wings. Nickel plated double bumper. Metal license plates. Drum type metal headlights with bar. Hood vents. Gear shift. Double windshield. Spotlight. Upholstered seat. Trunk. Large rubber pedals. Fenders and tail-light.

Wheels   10 in. double disc, roller bearings, with ⅝ inch rubber tires, nickel plated hub caps. See page seven.

Packed one in a crate, weight 70 lbs.

NO. 75RBD

Body   Length overall 42 inches. Wheelbase 30 inches. Easy riding springs on rear.

Finish   Green, striped in yellow and red. Fenders red. Wheels enameled red with green center and striped in green.

Equipment   Auto type molded rubber steering wheel with gas control lever. Horn. Instrument board. Motometer with wings. Nickel plated double bumper. Metal license plates. Glass headlights with bar. One-piece windshield. Spotlight. Hood vents. Gear shift. Upholstered seat. Large rubber pedals. Nickel plated radiator sheel of beautiful design. Oil can. Nickel plated kick plates. Rubber mats on running boards. Gas tank. Fenders and tail-light.

Wheels   10 in. double disc, roller bearings, with 1 inch rubber tires, nickel plated hub caps. See page seven.

Packed one in a crate, weight 70 lbs.

1927 Garton Catalog Page

NO. 69PBD

Body   Length overall 36 inches. Wheelbase 24 inches.

Finish   Red, striped and decorated in gold. Wheels enameled red.

Equipment   Auto type wood steering wheel with gas control lever. Bell. Instrument board. Bumper. License plate. Metal lamps. Gear shift. Gas tank. Rubber pedals. Fenders and tail-light.

Wheels   10 in. double disc, plain bearings, with ½ inch rubber tires, nickel plated hub caps.

Packed one in a crate, weight 48 lbs.

NO. 57RBD

Body   Length overall 42 inches. Wheelbase 30 inches.

Finish   Red, striped and decorated in yellow and black. Fenders red. Wheels red with green center and green stripes.

Equipment   Auto type molded rubber steering wheel with gas control lever. Horn. Instrument board. Motometer with wings. Bumper. Metal license plates. Drum type metal headlights with bar. Hood vents. Gear shift. One-piece windshield. Upholstered seat. Gas tank. Large rubber pedals. Fenders and tail-light.

Wheels   10 in. double disc, roller bearings with ⅝ inch rubber tires, nickel plated hub caps. See page seven.

Packed one in a crate, weight 60 lbs.

BADGER VELOCIPEDE WITH SIDE CAR

NO. 461SC VELOCIPEDE WITH SIDE CAR

Frame   Heavy, wide half-oval steel frame with malleable castings.
Handle Bars   Adjustable, nickel plated with rubber grips.
Saddle   Adjustable, padded top, leather bicycle saddle, with coil springs.
Wheels   Bright tin plated—Ball bearing, with nickel plated hub caps.
Front Wheel 16 inch, Rear Wheel 12 inch.
Pedals   Rubber. Pedals and cranks removable.
Tires   ¾ inch rubber.
Side Car   19 inches long, 12 inches wide and 6 inches deep. Well-shaped crowned fender over rear wheel, supporting side car.
Finish   Finished in attractive gray enamel and striped in red.

Packed one in a carton, weight 31 lbs.

NO. 53PBD

Body   Length overall 35 inches. Wheelbase 24 inches.
Finish   Red, striped and decorated in yellow and black. Wheels enameled red.
Equipment   Auto type wood steering wheel. Motometer. Instrument board. Bumper. License tag. Metal lamps. Rubber pedals.
Wheels   10 in. double disc, plain bearing, with 1¼ inch rubber tires, nickel plated hub caps.

Packed one in a carton, weight 31 lbs.

1927 Garton Catalog Page

NO. 52PBD

Body   Length overall 34 inches. Wheelbase 24 inches.
Finish   Royal blue, striped and decorated in yellow and black. Wheels enameled red.
Equipment   Auto type wood steering wheel. Motometer. License tag. Rubber pedals.
Wheels   10 in. double disc, plain bearing, with ½ inch rubber tires, nickel plated hub caps.

Packed one in a carton, weight 29 lbs.

No. 52PBW   Same as above except equipped with 10 inch wire wheels, plain bearing with ¾ inch rubber tires.

Packed one in a carton, weight 26 lbs.

NO. 76RBD

Body   Length overall 45 inches. Wheelbase 32 inches. Easy riding springs on rear.
Finish   Gray, striped in red and black. Fenders red, wheels enameled red with green center and striped in green.
Equipment   Auto type molded rubber steering wheel with gas control lever. Horn. Instrument board. Motometer with wings. Nickel plated double bumper. Metal license plates. Glass headlights with bar. Red and green sidelights. One-piece windshield. Spotlight. Hood vents. Gear shift. Upholstered seat. Nickel plated radiator shell of beautiful design. Trunk. Nickel plated kick plates. Rubber mats on running boards. Oil can. Fenders. Tail-light. Tool kit as shown on page seven.
Wheels   10 in. double disc, roller bearings, with 1 inch rubber tires, nickel plated hub caps. See page seven.

Packed one in a crate, weight 72 lbs.

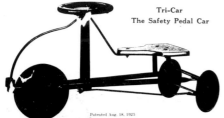

Tri-Car
The Safety Pedal Car

Patented Aug. 18, 1925

A new idea in a pedal car. The pedal wheel is always in a straight line—this prevents tipping, and it makes it more easily operated than the ordinary type of pedal car. The steering is done with an auto type steering wheel which turns the two rear wheels—this in itself is a novelty which appeals to the child. Of sturdy construction throughout. Attractively finished—green undergear—black steering wheel—ivory seat and red wheels. Heavy rubber bumper in front. Double disc wheels with rubber tires.

No.	Height to top of Seat	Length overall	Wheels	Tires	Weight per carton
443	8¾ in.	30½ in.	6 and 8 in.	½ in.	18 lbs.

Packed one in a carton

BADGER HAND CAR

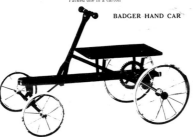

Seat made of selected hardwood, finished in red. Strong steel frame enameled black. Wire wheels, black enameled, equipped with rubber tires. Black enameled grips with nickel plated ferrules. Note No. 501 and 500 are Junior sizes.

No.	Length Overall	Wheels	Tires	Seat	Weight
500	28½ in.	8 and 10 in.	⅜ in.	7 x 12 in.	24 lbs.
501	28½ in.	8 and 10 in.	½ in.	7 x 12 in.	25 lbs.
502	36 in.	8 and 10 in.	½ in.	9 x 16 in.	30 lbs.

Packed one in a crate

BRONCHO HAND CAR

This hand car is larger than the Badger. Frame and handle made of selected hardwood, finished in red. Seatboard made of elm, natural varnished finish. Wire wheels, red enameled equipped with rubber tires. Black enameled grips with nickel plated ferrules.

No.	Length Overall	Wheels	Tires	Seat	Weight
503	41 in.	8 and 12 in.	½ in.	9 x 20 in.	37 lbs.

Packed one in a crate.

DISC WHEEL HAND CAR

Strong steel frame enameled black. Seat made of selected hardwood, finished in red Double disc, plain bearing wheels enameled red, equipped with rubber tires.

No.	Length Overall	Wheels	Tires	Seat	Weight
507	36 in.	8 and 10 in.	½ in.	9 x 16 in.	33 lbs.

Packed one in a crate

1927 Garton Catalog Page

NO. 55PBD

Body Length overall 35 inches. Wheelbase 24 inches.

Finish Tan, striped and decorated in red and black. Wheels enameled red.

Equipment Auto type wood steering wheel with gas control lever. Instrument board. Motometer. Bumper. License tag. Metal lamps. Rubber pedals.

Wheels 10 in. double disc, plain bearing, with ½ inch rubber tires, nickel plated hub caps.

Packed one in a carton, weight 32 lbs.

NO. 51PBW

Body Length overall 35 inches. Wheelbase 24 inches.

Finish Red, striped and decorated in black and yellow. Wheels enameled red.

Equipment Auto type wood steering wheel. Motometer. Bumper. License tag. Gas tank. Rubber pedals.

Wheels 8 in. wire, plain bearing, with ⅜ inch rubber tires, nickel plated hub caps.

Packed one in a carton, weight 25 lbs.

No. 50PBW Length overall 31 inches. Same as above, except without bumper, motometer and gas tank.

Packed one in a carton, weight 24 lbs.

NO. 67RBD

Body   Length overall 47 inches. Wheelbase 32 inches. Easy riding springs on rear.

Finish   Playboy blue striped and decorated in black and red. Fenders red. Wheels enameled red with green center and striped in green.

Equipment   Auto type molded rubber steering wheel with gas control lever. Horn. Instrument board. Motometer with wings. Nickel plated double bumper. Metal license plates. Glass headlights with bar. Red and green side lamps. Nickel plated radiator shell of beautiful design. Hood vents. Gear shift. Double windshield. Spotlight. Upholstered seat and back. Spare wheel on rear. Large rubber pedals. Oil can. Nickel plated kick plates. Rubber mats on running boards. Fenders and tail-light.

Wheels   10 in. double disc, roller bearings, with 1 inch rubber tires, nickel plated hub caps. See page seven.

Packed one in a crate, weight 72 lbs.

NO. 60PBD

Body   Length overall 45 inches. Wheelbase 32 inches.

Finish   Red, striped and decorated in yellow and black. Wheels enameled red.

Equipment   Auto type molded rubber steering wheel with gas control lever. Horn. Instrument board. Motometer. Bumper. License tag. Drum type metal headlights. Hood vents. Gear shift. Trunk. Rubber pedals.

Wheels   10 in. double disc, plain bearings with ½ inch rubber tires, nickel plated hub caps.

Packed one in a carton, weight 46 lbs.

1927 Garton Catalog Page

NO. 72PBD

Body   Length overall 45 inches. Wheelbase 32 inches. Easy riding springs on rear.

Finish   Tan, striped and decorated in red and black. Wheels enameled red.

Equipment   Auto type molded rubber steering wheel with gas control lever. Horn. Instrument board. Motometer with wings. Bumper. Metal license plates. Drum type metal headlights with bar. Hood vents. Gear shift. Rubber pedals. Nickel plated radiator shell of beautiful design. Trunk.

Wheels   10 in. double disc, plain bearings, with ½ inch rubber tires, nickel plated hub caps.

Packed one in a carton, weight 48 lbs.

NO. 73PBD

Body   Length overall 41 inches. Wheelbase 30 inches. Easy riding springs on rear.

Finish   Tan, striped and decorated in red and black. Fenders black. Wheels enameled red.

Equipment   Auto type molded rubber steering wheel with gas control lever. Horn. Instrument board. Motometer with wings. Bumper. Metal license plates. Drum type metal headlights with bar. One-piece windshield. Spotlight. Gear shift. Large rubber pedals. Nickel plated radiator shell of beautiful design. Nickel plated kick plates. Rubber mats on running boards. Oil can. Fenders and tail-light.

Wheels   10 in. double disc, plain bearings with ½ inch rubber tires, nickel plated hub caps.

Packed one in a crate, weight 63 lbs.

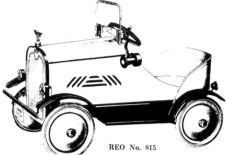

Body Length overall 36 inches. Wheelbase 25 inches.
Finish Cream, striped green and red. Wheels cream, striped green. Fenders black.
Equipment As shown. With instrument board.
Wheels 10 in. disc, plain bearing. ¾ in. rubber tires. Nickel plated hub caps.
Packing One in crate. Weight 52 lbs.

REO No. 815

SPEEDWAGON DUMP TRUCK No. 831
Body Length overall 50 inches. Wheelbase 32 inches. Box 15x13x5½ inches. Rear of box hinged.
Finish Baked enamel. Green, striped red and yellow. Wheels green. Fenders red.
Equipment As shown. With instrument board. Lever to raise dump platform.
Wheels 10 in. disc, roller bearing. ¾ in. rubber tires. Nickel plated hub caps.
Packing One in crate. Weight 66 lbs.

Body Length overall 38 inches. Wheelbase 26 inches. Springs on rear.
Finish Baked enamel. Canary yellow and blue, striped red, blue and yellow. Wheels yellow with blue center, striped red. Fenders blue, striped yellow.
Equipment As shown. With instrument board.
Wheels 10 in. disc, plain bearing. ¾ in. rubber tires. Nickel plated hub caps.
Packing One in crate. Weight 52 lbs.

MARMON No. 816

DIAMOND T DUMP TRUCK No. 832
Body Length overall 50 inches. Wheelbase 32 inches. Box 15x15x5½ inches. Rear of box hinged.
Finish Baked enamel. Gray, striped green and red. Wheels gray with red centers. Fenders red.
Equipment As shown. With instrument board. Lever to raise dump platform.
Wheels 10 in. disc, roller bearing. 1⅛ in. rubber tires. Nickel plated hub caps.
Packing One in crate. Weight 86 lbs.

1930 Garton

PONTIAC No. 812
Body Length overall 32 inches. Wheelbase 21 inches.
Finish Baked enamel. Body light brilliant green, striped black and cream. Wheels cream, green striped.
Equipment As shown.
Wheels 8 in. disc, plain bearing. ½ inch rubber tires. Nickel plated hub caps.
Packing One in carton. Weight 48 lbs.

KISSEL No. 819
Body Length overall 45 inches. Wheelbase 30 inches.
Finish Marmon striped black and yellow. Wheels marmon, striped yellow. Fenders marmon.
Equipment As shown. With instrument board. Springs on rear.
Wheels 10 in. disc, roller bearing. 1 in. rubber tires. Nickel plated hub caps.
Packing One in crate. Weight 76 lbs.

CADILLAC No. 821
Body Length overall 51½ inches. Wheelbase 37 inches.
Finish Baked enamel. Body ivory and blue, striped red and black. Wheels blue, striped red. Fenders black.
Equipment As shown. With instrument board. Large rubber pedals. Hinged door. Springs on rear.
Wheels 10 in. balloon type disc, roller bearing. 1 in. rubber tires. Nickel plated hub caps.
Packing One in crate. Weight 90 lbs.

PACKARD No. 814
Body Length overall 36 inches. Wheelbase 24 inches.
Finish Baked enamel. Body light blue, striped black and red. Wheels cream, striped blue. Fenders black.
Equipment As shown. With instrument board.
Wheels 10 in. disc, plain bearing. ½ inch rubber tires. Nickel plated hub caps.
Packing One in carton. Weight 50 lbs.

NASH No. 825

Body Length overall 30 inches. Wheelbase 21 inches.
Finish Baked enamel. Body red, striped gold. Wheels red, striped gold.
Equipment As shown.
Wheels 8 in. plain bearing. ½ in. rubber tires. Nickel plated hub caps.
Packing One in carton. Weight 30 lbs.

BUICK No. 813

Body Length overall 34 inches. Wheelbase 23 inches.
Finish Baked enamel. Body light blue, striped red and black. Wheels cream, striped blue.
Equipment As shown. With instrument board.
Wheels 10 in. disc, plain bearing. ¾ in. rubber tires. Nickel plated hub caps.
Packing One in carton. Weight 32 lbs.

Page Thirty-Nine

BADGER AEROPLANES

U. S. AIRMAIL NO. 834
(All Steel)

Body Length overall 42 inches. Wheelbase 33 inches. Wing 30x9 inches. Propeller 14x3 inches.
Finish Baked enamel. Body orange. Wing, seat, fins, tail, propeller black. Decorations orange.
Equipment As shown.
Wheels Front 8 in., rear 6 in. Plain bearing. ½ in. rubber tires. Nickel plated hub caps.
Packing One in crate. Weight 53 lbs.

NO. 425 MONOPLANE

Size Length overall 34 inches. Wheelbase 19 inches. Wing 20x7 inches. Propeller 11x2½ inches. Seat, fin, propeller, wing, hardwood. Undergear heavy steel. Pedals rubber.

Finish Enamel. Seat green. Seat back and wing ivory. Propeller varnished natural. Decorations red and blue.

Wheels Front 10 in. disc. Rear 6 in. disc. Plain bearing ⅛ in rubber tires.

Packing Two in carton. Weight 32 lbs.

Page Forty-Six

1930 Garton

BADGER AEROPLANE

SWALLOW NO. 836
(All Steel)

Body Length overall 47 inches. Wheelbase 33 inches. Wing 30x9 inches. Propeller 14x3 inches.

Finish Baked enamel. Body tan. Wing, fin, tail and nose green. Decorations orange. Propeller, cylinders and wing braces nickel plated. Undergear black.

Equipment As shown.

Wheels Front 10 in., balloon type, rear 8 in. Roller bearing. 1¼ in. rubber tires. Nickel plated hub caps.

Packing One in crate. Weight 65 lbs.

BADGER AEROPLANE

CURTISS ROBIN NO. 835
(All Steel)

Body Length overall 47 inches. Wheelbase 33 inches. Wing 30x9 inches. Propeller 14x3 inches.

Finish Baked enamel. Body blue. Wings, fins, tail red. Propeller, cylinders black. Decorations yellow.

Equipment As shown.

Wheels Front 10 in., rear 8 in. Roller bearing. ¾ in. rubber tires. Nickel plated hub caps.

Packing One in crate. Weight 60 lbs.

Page Forty-Eight

Page Forty-Seven

POLICE PATROL NO. 829

Body   Length overall 49 inches. Wheelbase 31 inches.
Finish   Baked enamel. Body blue, striped gold. Wheels blue, striped gold. Fenders red, striped black.
Equipment   As shown. With instrument board. Bell under hood.
Wheels   10 in. disc, roller bearing. 1 in. rubber tires. Nickel plated hub caps.
Packing   One in crate. Weight 71 lbs.

HOOK AND LADDER NO. 827

Body   Length overall 49 inches. Wheelbase 32 inches.
Finish   Baked enamel. Red, striped gold. Wheels red, striped gold.
Equipment   As shown. With instrument board. Ladders 26 inches long.
Wheels   10 in. disc, roller bearing. 1 in. rubber tires. Nickel plated hub caps.
Packing   One in crate. Weight 74 lbs.

Page Forty-Four

FORD No. 810

Body   Length overall 30 inches. Wheelbase 21 inches.
Finish   Baked enamel. Body red, striped black and yellow. Wheels red.
Equipment   As shown.
Wheels   8 in. wire, plain bearing. ⅞ in. rubber tires. Nickel plated hub caps.
Packing   One in carton. Weight 24 lbs.

CHEVROLET No. 811

Body   Length overall 30 inches. Wheelbase 21 inches.
Finish   Baked enamel. Body green, striped black and cream. Wheels cream with green stripes.
Equipment   As shown.
Wheels   8 in. disc, plain bearing. ½ in. rubber tires. Nickel plated hub caps.
Packing   One in carton. Weight 28 lbs.

Page Thirty-Eight

1930 Garton

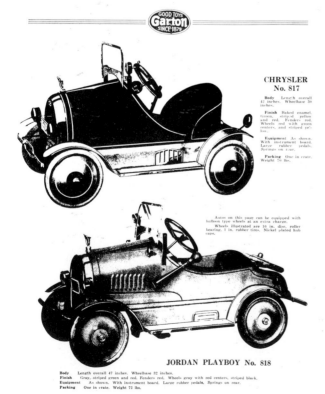

CHRYSLER No. 817

Body   Length overall 42 inches. Wheelbase 30 inches.

Finish   Baked enamel. Green, striped yellow and red. Fenders red. Wheels red with green centers, and striped yellow.

Equipment   As shown. With instrument board. Large rubber pedals. Springs on rear.

Packing   One in crate. Weight 70 lbs.

Autos on this page can be equipped with balloon type wheels at an extra charge.
Wheels illustrated are 10 in. disc, roller bearing. 1 in. rubber tires. Nickel plated hub caps.

JORDAN PLAYBOY No. 818

Body   Length overall 47 inches. Wheelbase 32 inches.
Finish   Gray, striped green and red. Fenders red. Wheels gray with red centers, striped black.
Equipment   As shown. With instrument board. Large rubber pedals. Springs on rear.
Packing   One in crate. Weight 72 lbs.

Page Forty-Two

FORD DUMP TRUCK No. 830

Body   Length overall 47 inches. Wheelbase 26 inches. Box 15x14x5½ inches. Rear of box hinged.
Finish   Baked enamel. Red, striped green and yellow. Wheels red.
Equipment   As shown. With instrument board. Lever to raise dump platform.
Wheels   8 in. disc, plain bearing. ½ in. rubber tires. Nickel plated hub caps.
Packing   One in carton. Weight 33 lbs.

LA SALLE No. 820

Body   Length overall 50 inches. Wheelbase 37 inches. Springs on rear.
Finish   Baked enamel. Body tan, striped black and orange. Wheel rims burnt orange, striped black. Fenders tan, striped orange.
Equipment   As shown. With instrument board. Oil can. Large rubber pedals.
Wheels   10 in. ball bearing. Rust-proof cadmium plated tangent spokes and nipples. 1⅛ in. tires. Nickel plated hub caps.
Packing   One in crate. Weight 86 lbs.

Page Forty-Five

18

FOUR STAR FEATURE

$9⁶⁹ FREE!
WITH AUTO
GOGGLES AND HELMET

Save $3.00 on This
New Streamliner

You can bet all the gang will be green-eyed when they see you in this big car. Its classy lines gracefully show its sturdiness and smooth flowing beauty like that of the newest motor cars. Built to last for many a happy tour. Goggles and helmet free with this auto.

For Tots Up to 7 Yrs.

Heavy auto-fender steel body and beautifully sweeping fenders are one piece to give strength. Sports mode windshield. Streamline radiator ornament adds a touch of quality. Such features as ball bearing driveshafts, adjustable rubber pedals, seat pad, new type double bar bumper, insure comfort and longer life. Dummy headlights and gleaming red baked-on enamel finish. Artillery type roller bearing 9½-inch double disc steel wheels, with ¾-inch rubber tires. Large dome hub caps. Length, 42 in.; width, 17 in. Shipping weight, 37 pounds. **Not mailable.**

79 VM 8954—Complete....**$9.69**

Super Features on Two Prize Winners:

WILL HOLD TWO MEN

BALL BEARING DRIVE SHAFTS

THREE ADJUSTMENTS ON FOOT PEDALS

Hotter'n Hot!
And Boy! What a Price!

53-Inch supercharger! Newest thing on wheels—designed by America's foremost auto designer. Gleaming ivory color exhaust pipes set off the fine, aristocratic Dubonnet (maroon) baked-on finish on body and sweeping fenders.

For Kids Up to 10 Yrs.

Double bar bumper—new style windshield, colorful dummy instrument board—dummy headlights. 10-in. roller bearing, artillery wheels, ¾-in. rubber tires. large dome hub caps. Fiber covered seat, bulb horn. Enjoy a **cushioned ride** with the ball bearing drive shafts, spring type chassis. Adjustable rubber pedals. 53 in. long, 18 in. wide. Shpg. wt., 62 lbs. Not mailable.
79 VM 8956....**$14.95**

$20 Value
$14⁹⁵

SHOCK ABSORBING REAR SPRINGS

ACTUALLY DUMPS

Save $2.00 on This Big Mack
44½-In. Real Dump Truck—For Tots Up to 8 Yrs.

With all the road-building going on, you'll need a big dump truck like this to get your share of the business. And here's a truck that "can take it"—heavy steel throughout. **Every inch a Mack** with big dump box, 15 in. long, 14 in. wide, 5 in. deep. Large dome hub caps on 8½-in. steel artillery wheels, with ⅝-in. rubber tires. Finished in red baked-on enamel, nicely decorated. Adjustable rubber pedals, **spring type chassis absorbs all jars. 44½ in. long, 20 in. wide. Mailable.** Shpg. wt., 38 lbs.
79 V 8960
Big Mack.$7.98

$7⁹⁸

Sports Roadster Save 25%
All-Steel 1-Pc. Body—For Tots Up to 6 Yrs

A car that any young motorist will be proud to run. **Just as strong as it is good-looking** because **body** and **fenders** are **all steel in one piece.** Finished in attractive Dubonnet (maroon) baked-on enamel with contrasting ivory striping. Completely fitted with such accessories as fancy radiator ornament, latest divided type windshield, bulb horn, and dummy streamlined lights. 8¼-in. steel artillery wheels; ⅝-in. rubber tires. 35½ in. long and 15½ in. wide. Rubber pedals. **Mailable.**
79 V 8953—Shpg. wt., 30 lbs...**$7.48**

$7⁴⁸

Fire Chief Auto and Hat
A $7 Value. For Tots Up to 5 Yrs.

Clang! Clang! Make way for the young fireman. The nickeled bell clanging with every pull of the cord will stop all sidewalk traffic and the flashing real "fire-engine" red, all steel body will attract every eye. And think of it! **A fire chief hat free with every car.** Sturdily built for years of alarms—size overall, 33½x15 inches. 8¼-inch double disc steel wheels, ½-inch rubber tires. Rubber pedals. **Mailable.** Shipping weight, 27 pounds.
79 V 8952...............**$5.48**

$5⁴⁸

GLOBE
Tred-l-bike

THE FIRST REALLY PRACTICAL, SUCCESSFUL

mechanical scooter

No. 2000

successor to the "SIDEWALK BIKE"

IT PROPELS with a simple rocking motion.

IT COASTS Free-wheeling—usable as a coaster alone.

IT SPEEDS at a surprising rate—easy to ride —no instructions required.

and IT WORKS —simple, practical, with nothing to get out of order—absolutely safe.

★ THE AGE LIMIT FOR SCOOTERS NOW GOES UP FROM 6 TO 10

This new invention (patented) opens up an important new market for wheel goods. The child gets on and rides it THE FIRST TIME, without instruction. It satisfies his urge to ride on two wheels, but it costs only a fraction of the price of a "side-walk bike"—which thousands never can afford to buy. It is just what you have always

needed in your wheel goods line, to bridge the gap between velocipedes and full-size bicycles. ● As another step in its program to give you distinctive, salable merchandise AT THE TOP OF THE LINE, where the profits are, Globe is proud to present the Tred-L-Bike, its first mechanical scooter and, we sincerely believe, the first one to be perfected. Priced to be within reach of every child.

SPECIFICATIONS FOR TRED-L-BIKE

Size—Length 48", height 33". **Footboard**—Wood, 4¼"x19". **Pedal Board**—Steel, 5¾"x15¾", covered with molded rubber. **Wheels**—Automotive type ball bearing. **Drive**—Rack and pinion drive with internal over-running clutch. Drive and internal parts of case hardened steel. **Handle Bar**—Tubular steel with rubber grips. **Equipment**—Brake, parking stand, bell and fender. **Color**—Standard color, red. Green and tan optional. **Packing**—One in corrugated shipping carton.

No.	Wheels	Tires	Weight
2000	12"	1"	30

 Globe OF SHEBOYGAN

No. 2520

Body—One-piece steel. **Finish**—Blue enamel baked on. Red or green optional. Can be finished in green and white, or other two-tone combinations at small extra cost. **Equipment**—Canvas knee pad, nickel plated side rails, bumper and handle. **Wheels**—Spoke type, ball bearing. **Packing**—One in a corrugated shipping carton.

No.	Body Size	Wheels	Tires	Axles	Weight
2520	16½x34½x4¾"	10"	1"	½"	37

Can be equipped with Brake as shown on **No. 2511.**

No. 2520
Ball Bearing Equipped

No. 2512
No. 2515
Ball Bearing Equipped

No. 2512

Body—One-piece steel. **Finish**—Red enamel baked on. Blue or green optional. Can be finished in two-tone combinations at small extra cost. **Equipment**—Canvas knee pad or seat, nickel plated double rails, bumper and handle. **Wheels**—Ball bearing with pneumatic tires. **Packing**—One in a corrugated shipping carton.

No. 2515 is same as **No. 2512** except disc wheels.

No.	Body Size	Wheels	Tires	Axles	Weight
2512	16½x34½x4¾"	10"	2¾"	½"	42
2515	16½x34½x4¾"	10"	1"	½"	43

Can be equipped with Brake as shown on **No. 2511.**

No. 2514

Body—One-piece steel. **Finish**—Blue enamel baked on. Green or red optional. Can be finished in two-tone combinations at small extra cost. **Equipment**—Canvas knee pad, nickel plated side rails, bumper and handle. **Wheels**—Ball bearing with pneumatic tires. **Packing**—One in a corrugated shipping carton.

No.	Body Size	Wheels	Tires	Axles	Weight
2514	16½x34½x4¾"	10"	2¾"	½"	37½

No. 2514
Ball Bearing Equipped

5738

Body—Length overall 43 inches. **Finish**—Baked enamel. Body and wheels red decorated white and black. **Equipment**—Electric headlights, less battery. Fire bell. Bumper. Adjustable pedals. Varnished ladders and step on rear. **Gear**—Roller bearing legs and drive shafts at rear. **Wheels**—9 inch 12 spoke artillery. ⅝ inch tires. Balloon hub caps. **Packing**—One in carton. Weight 49 pounds.

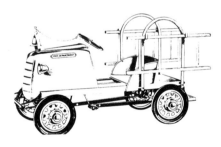

AUTOMOBILES

5716

OLDSMOBILE

Body—Length overall 39 inches. **Finish**—Baked enamel. Body Riviera blue decorated white, windshield white. Wheels white striped blue and black. **Equipment**—One piece fenders and running board welded to body. Headlights non-electric. Plated bumper. Windshield. **Gear**—Roller bearing legs at rear. Adjustable pedals. **Wheels**—9 in. 12 spoke artillery. ⅝ inch tires. Balloon hub caps. **Packing**—One in carton ready for easy assembly. Weight 44 pounds.

Note:—Artillery wheels now standard equipment.

Globe OF SHEBOYGAN

GARTON TOY COMPANY

5774
LINCOLN ZEPHYR

Body—Length overall 45 inches. Special pointed front. **Finish**—Baked enamel. Body manila tan decorated ivory, striped red and black. **Equipment**—Plated electric headlights less battery. One piece fenders with running board and apron. Bumper. Metal instrument board. **Gear**—Roller bearing legs and drive shaft at rear. Adjustable pedals. **Wheels**—9-inch 12 spoke artillery. ⅝-inch tires. Balloon hub caps. **Packing**—One in carton. Weight 53 pounds.

Note:—Artillery wheels now standard equipment.

AUTOMOBILES

5778
LA SALLE

Body—Length overall 48 inches. **Finish**—Baked enamel. Body white decorated green striped red. Fenders green. Wheels white striped green and black. **Equipment**—Electric headlights less battery. Windshield equipped with wiper. Horn. Metal instrument board. Bumper. One piece fenders with running board and apron. **Gear**—Roller bearing legs and drive shafts at rear. Adjustable pedals. **Wheels**—9½-inch 12 spoke roller bearing artillery. ¾-inch tires. Balloon hub caps. **Packing**—One in carton. Weight 55 pounds.

Note:—Artillery wheels now standard equipment.

GARTON TOY COMPANY

SCOOTERS AUTOMOBILES

5802
Ride-Em-Cowboy

Size—Length 22½ inches. Height overall 22½ inches. Height of seat from floor 15½ inches. **Wheels**—Ball bearing roller skate wheels. Shock absorbing rubber cushions on trucks. **Construction**—Frame of ⅝-inch steel tubing. Handle of wood. Streamlined steel footboard. Metal saddle. **Finish**—Baked enamel. Footboard and seat red. Frame and handle ivory decorated black. **Packing**—Four in carton. **Weight**—Per carton 31 pounds.

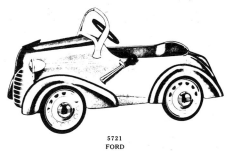

5721
FORD

Body—Length overall 39 inches. Fenders attached to body. **Finish**—Baked enamel. Body red decorated ivory. Wheels ivory striped red. Windshield ivory. **Equipment**—Headlights non-electric. Windshield. Horn. Radiator ornament. Adjustable pedals. **Gear**—Roller bearing legs. **Wheels**—8-inch artillery. ⅝-inch tires. **Packing**—One in carton. Weight—44 pounds.

5803

Size—Length 30 inches, height 28 inches. Streamlined steel footboard. **Wheels**—7-inch double disc. ⅜-inch rubber tires. **Finish**—Baked red enamel. **Equipment**—Parking stand. **Packing**—Six in carton. **Weight**—Per carton 47 pounds.

5722
FORD

Body—Length overall 39 inches. Fenders attached to body. **Finish**—Baked enamel. Body red decorated white. Wheels white striped red. **Equipment**—Headlights non-electric. Fire bell. Adjustable pedals. **Gear**—Roller bearing legs. **Wheels**—8 inch artillery. ⅝-inch tires. **Packing**—One in carton. **Weight**—44 pounds.

SHEBOYGAN, WISCONSIN

GARTON TOY COMPANY

THE NEXT 15 PAGES

1941
STEELCRAFT

Designed by Victor Schreckengost

R. A. F. Spitfire Plane

Model No. B697

(For Children 3 to 7 Years)

SPECIFICATIONS

OVERALL DIMENSIONS: Length, 45½″. Width of body, 13½″. Wing spread, 35″.

WHEELS: 10″ double disc, beaded type, with 1¾″ semi-pneumatic tires on front. 8″ with ⅝″ tire on rear.

EQUIPMENT: Propeller that turns when plane is propelled, windshield, and two dummy machine guns and an airplane cannon mounted over motor.

FINISH: Body in Hazelwood Brown baked enamel with Orange trim. Undergear in Black. Wings and wheels in Orange. Windshield, guns and propeller chrome plated.

PACKED: One to a carton.   SHIPPING WEIGHT: 46 lbs.

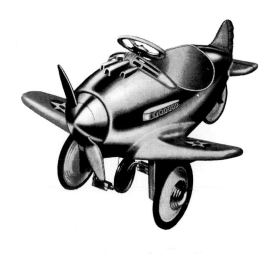

THESE NEW JUVENILE AIRPLANE MODELS ARE DE-SIGNED ALONG THE LONG RACY STREAMLINES SIMILAR TO THE MOST MODERN PURSUIT SHIPS NOW IN USE. A GREAT DEAL OF CARE AND EXPENSE HAVE BEEN EXERCISED IN MAKING THESE BONA FIDE REPRODUCTIONS.

Designed by Viktor Schreckengost

U. S. Pursuit Plane
Model No. B695
(For Children 3 to 7 Years)
SPECIFICATIONS

OVERALL DIMENSIONS: Length 45½″. Width of body 13½″. Wing spread 35″.

WHEELS: 10″ beaded type, with ¾″ rubber tires on front. 8″ with ⅝″ tire on rear.

EQUIPMENT: Propeller that turns when plane is pedaled, windshield, and two dummy machine guns and an airplane cannon mounted over motor.

FINISH: Body, wings and windshield in Silver baked enamel with Vermilion and Blue trim. Undergear in Black. Wheels in Red.

PACKED: One in a carton.   **SHIPPING WEIGHT:** 45 lbs.

SELDOM HAS IT BEEN OUR PLEASURE TO BRING OUT A MORE DISTINGUISHED INNOVATION IN THE WHEEL GOODS LINE. THIS NEW AIRPLANE, IN KEEPING WITH THE TIMES, REPRESENTS THE LAST WORD IN STYLE.

Star Automobile

Model No. B540

(Children 2 to 5 Years)

SPECIFICATIONS

OVERALL DIMENSIONS: Length 35"; width 15½".

WHEELS: 8" beaded type with large Silver hub caps and ⅝" rubber tires.

EQUIPMENT: Motometer, seat pad.

FINISH: Body in Green with White trim. Wheels in White. Steering wheel in Black.

PACKED: One to a carton. Weight: 29 lbs.

Model No. B540

1-Ton
Mack Hook and Ladder

Model No. B680

(For Children 3 to 6 Years)

SPECIFICATIONS

OVERALL DIMENSIONS: With ladders—length, 50½"; width, 20".

OVERALL DIMENSIONS: Without ladders—length, 40¾"; width, 20".

LENGTH OF LADDERS: (2)—27" each.

WHEELS: 8" Double disc, artillery type, with ⅝" rubber tires, with dome plated hub caps.

EQUIPMENT: Two five-rung ladders, Red and Green lanterns, fire bell, hand rails, and back step for second child.

FINISH: Body and hood in Red baked enamel with Ivory trim. Wheels in Ivory. Ladders varnished and Red striped. Hand rails in Silver.

PACKED: One in a carton. WEIGHT: 42 lbs.

Model No. B680

Junior Service Truck

Model No. B643

(For Children 2 to 5 Years)

SPECIFICATIONS

OVERALL DIMENSIONS: Length, 44½″; width, 15½″.

WHEELS: 8″ beaded disc with silver hub caps and ⅝″ rubber tires.

EQUIPMENT: 2 hand rails, windlass with cord and hook, windshield, bumper, bulb horn, motometer and seat pad.

FINISH: Body and chassis in White baked enamel with Red trim. Box and wheels in Red. Hand rails, bumper and windlass in silver.

PACKED: One to a carton. WEIGHT: 35 lbs.

Model No. B643

GREATEST IN PLAY VALUES

Buick Fire Chief Auto

Model No. B565

(For Children 3 to 6 Years)

SPECIFICATIONS

OVERALL DIMENSIONS: Length, 41½″; width, 17½″.

WHEELS: 8″ double disc with ⅝″ black rubber tires. Beaded type, with large beaded hub caps.

EQUIPMENT: Fire Chief bell, pull cord, bumper, seat pad, chrome headlights and windshield.

FENDERS: Front and rear are an integral part of the body.

FINISH: Body in Red, with White trim. Wheels in White. Bumper, steering wheel and windshield in Silver.

PACKING: One to carton. WEIGHT: 40 lbs.

Special construction reduces set-up work to minimum.

Model No. B565

GREATEST IN PLAY VALUES

The Super Charger

Model No. B620

(For Children 4 to 9 years)

THE time is ripe for a real De Luxe Juvenile Automobile. This model has as fine lines as any large auto of today. It is a standout for value; no dealer can afford to be without this model.

SPECIFICATIONS

OVERALL DIMENSIONS: Length 53″. Width 18″.

WHEELS: 10″ roller bearing double disc wheels with 1″ rubber tires, artillery type.

FENDERS: Are an integral part of body, both body and fenders are made of twenty gauge steel.

EQUIPMENT: New double leaf bumper, new style windshield, designed instrument board, ball bearing spring type chassis, French bulb horn, exhaust pipes on side, Black seat and back pads, bumper, steering wheel, windshield, exhaust pipes and radiator ornament.

FINISH: Body is in Maroon baked enamel with White trim. Wheels in White. Bumper, steering wheel, windshield, exhaust pipes and radiator ornament are all chromium plated.

PACKED: One in carton. SHIPPING WEIGHT: 60 lbs.

Style of construction reduces set-up to minimum.

Super Charger DeLuxe

Model No. B630

(For Children 4 to 9 years)

Unless you see one of these models you cannot appreciate what a real Juvenile Automobile should look like. This model has paved the way for the retail sale of higher priced automobiles.

SPECIFICATIONS

OVERALL DIMENSIONS: Length, 53″. Width, 18″.

WHEELS: 10″ ball bearing with 2¾″ White sidewall pneumatic tires.

FENDERS: Are an integral part of body, both body and fenders are made of twenty gauge steel.

EQUIPMENT: New double leaf bumper, new style windshield, designed instrument board, ball bearing spring type chassis, French bulb horn, exhaust pipes on side, Red seat and back pads, bumper, steering wheel, windshield, exhaust pipes and radiator ornament.

FINISH: Body is in Black Baked Enamel with Red trim. Wheels in Red. Bumper, steering wheel, windshield, exhaust pipes and radiator ornament are all chromium plated.

PACKED: One in carton. SHIPPING WEIGHT: 58 lbs.

Style of construction reduces set-up to minimum.

The Streamliner

Model No. B600

(For Children 4 to 9 Years)

HERE is a Juvenile Auto built of twenty gauge automobile steel, incorporating the finest lines ever seen on an auto of this kind. Ultra modern in appearance—large in size and priced to sell in a popular retail bracket.

SPECIFICATIONS

OVERALL DIMENSIONS: Length, 53″. Width, 18″.

WHEELS: 10″ roller bearing, double disc wheels—artillery type, with ¾″ rubber tires.

FENDERS: Are an integral part of body, both body and fenders are made of twenty gauge steel.

EQUIPMENT: New double leaf bumper, new style windshield, designed instrument board, ball bearing spring type chassis, French bulb horn, long lamp bodies on side, seat pad and radiator ornaments.

FINISH: Body in Green baked enamel with Ivory trim. Bumper, head lights, windshield and wheels in Ivory.

PACKED: One in carton. SHIPPING WEIGHT: 58 lbs.

Style of construction reduces set-up to minimum.

Chrysler Airflow

Model No. B580

(For Children 3 to 8 Years)

SPECIFICATIONS

OVERALL DIMENSIONS: Length, 43¾″; width, 18″.

WHEELS: 10″ Roller bearing, artillery type with ¾″ rubber tires and large plated dome hub caps.

EQUIPMENT: Headlamps, French bulb horn, front bumper, windshield, ball bearing spring type chassis, adjustable rubber pedals, Chrysler radiator ornament and steering wheel. The fenders and running boards are part of the body.

FINISH: Body in Maroon baked enamel with Ivory trim.   Wheels, steering wheel, bumper, windshield, headlights in Ivory.

PACKING: One to carton.

SHIPPING WEIGHT: 50 lbs.

The construction of this Auto reduces set-up work to a minimum.

Zephyr Automobile

Model No. B579

(For Children 3 to 6 Years)

The "tops" in Juvenile Automobile design and construction. Sold to retail in a popular price bracket, this item has everything to appeal to the child.

SPECIFICATIONS

OVERALL DIMENSIONS: Length 42½"; Width 17½".

WHEELS: 10" new style double disc, roller bearing with ¾" tires. New style hub caps.

EQUIPMENT: Headlamps, French bulb horn, front bumper, windshield, adjustable rubber pedals, radiator ornament, seat pad and steering wheel. Fenders are a part of body.

FINISH: Body in Hazelwood Brown baked enamel with Orange trim. Wheels and headlamps in Orange. Windshield, steering wheel and bumper in Silver.

PACKING: One in carton. SHIPPING WEIGHT: 45 lbs.

Construction reduces dealer's set-up to a minimum.

Model No. B575

Same as above only finished in Red, with Ivory trim. Wheels and headlamps in Ivory. Windshield, steering wheel and bumper in silver.

Model No. B576

Same as above only finished in Maroon with Ivory trim. Wheels and headlamps in Ivory. Windshield, steering wheel and bumper in silver.

Model No. B550

Pontiac Automobile

Model No. B550

(For Children 2 to 5 Years)

SPECIFICATIONS

OVERALL DIMENSIONS: Length 35"; width 15½".

WHEELS: 8" beaded disc with large silver beaded hub caps and ⅝" rubber tires.

EQUIPMENT: Motometer, bell, horn, new windshield and seat pad.

FINISH: Body in Blue baked enamel with Ivory trim. Windshield, steering wheel in Ivory. Wheels in Red.

PACKING: One to a carton. Weight: 31 lbs.

Pontiac Fire Chief

Model No. B555

(For Children 2 to 5 Years)

SPECIFICATIONS

OVERALL DIMENSIONS: Length 35"; width 15½".

WHEELS: Beaded disc with large silver beaded hub caps and ⅝" rubber tires.

EQUIPMENT: Fire Chief bell and cord, new windshield and seat pad.

FINISH: Body in red baked enamel with ivory trim. Wheels, windshield in ivory. Steering wheel in black.

PACKING: One to a carton. WEIGHT: 31 lbs.

Model No. B555

Model No. B500

Ace Automobile

Model No. B500

(Children 1 to 3 Years)

SPECIFICATIONS

OVERALL DIMENSIONS: Length 31¼"; width .

WHEELS: New 8" beaded disc wheels with large
and ½" solid rubber tires.

EQUIPMENT: Motometer.

FINISH: Body in Red with Ivory trim. Wheels in Ivory Silver
hub caps.

PACKED: One to a carton. WEIGHT: 22 lbs.

Ace Fire Chief Auto

Model No. B502

(Children 1 to 3 Years)

SPECIFICATIONS

OVERALL DIMENSIONS: Length 31¼"; width 15½".

WHEELS: New 8" beaded disc wheels with large beaded hub
caps and ½" solid rubber tires.

EQUIPMENT: Fire Chief Bell with pull cord.

FINISH: Body in Red with Ivory trim. Wheels in Ivory with
Silver hub caps.

PACKED: One to a carton. WEIGHT: 22 lbs.

Model No. B502

GREATEST IN PLAY VALUES

Model No. B640

Junior Hook and Ladder

Model No. B640

(For Children 2 to 5 Years)

SPECIFICATIONS

OVERALL DIMENSIONS—With Ladders—
Length, 44″; width, 15½″

OVERALL DIMENSIONS—Without Ladders—
Length, 40″; width, 15½

WHEELS: 8″ beaded disc with Silver hub caps and ⅝″ rubber tires.

EQUIPMENT: 2 ladders, 2 hand rails, bell, bumper, windshield and seat pad.

FINISH: Body and chassis in Red baked enamel with White trim. Wheels in White, and hand rails and bumper in Silver.

PACKED: One in a carton. Weight: 34 lbs.

Junior Station Wagon

Model No. B641

(For Children 2 to 5 Years)

SPECIFICATIONS

OVERALL DIMENSIONS: Length, 44½″; width, 15½″.

WHEELS: 8″ beaded disc with Silver hub caps, and ⅝″ rubber tires.

EQUIPMENT: 2 hand rails, tail gate, windshield, bumper, bulb horn, motometer and seat pad.

FINISH: Body and chassis in Maroon baked enamel with Ivory trim. Box in Hazelwood Brown; wheels in Ivory and hand rails and bumper in Silver.

PACKED: One in a carton. WEIGHT: 34 lbs.

Model No. B641

GREATEST IN PLAY VALUES

Model No. B665

Air Flow Dump Truck

Model No. B665

(For Children 3 to 7 Years)

SPECIFICATIONS

OVERALL DIMENSIONS: Length, 50″; width, 18″.

WHEELS: 10″ Roller bearing, artillery type, with ¾″ Black rubber tires and large dome plated hub caps.

EQUIPMENT: Dual dumping mechanism, ball bearing spring type chassis, adjustable pedals, French bulb horn, bumper, radiator ornament, seat pad.

FINISH: Body in Maroon baked enamel with Ivory trim. Box and wheels in Ivory.

PACKING: One in a carton. WEIGHT: 56 lbs.

Model No. B675

Air Flow Fire Truck

This Auto Seats Two Children

Model No. B675

(For Children 3 to 7 Years)

SPECIFICATIONS

OVERALL DIMENSIONS: Length, 55″; width, 18″.

WHEELS: 10″ Roller bearing wheels, artillery type, with ¾″ Black rubber tires. Large dome type plated hub caps.

EQUIPMENT: Fire Chief bell, motometer, bumper, springs, Red and Green lanterns, two five-rung ladders, ball bearing chassis, adjustable pedals, rear seat and step. Tubular hand rails.

FINISH: In Red baked enamel with Ivory trim. Wheels in Ivory. Hand rails in Silver.

PACKING: One in a carton. WEIGHT: 56 lbs.

GREATEST IN PLAY VALUES

Eagle Roadster

Model No. B505

(Children 2 to 4 Years)

SPECIFICATIONS

OVERALL DIMENSIONS: Length 33½″; width 17″.

WHEELS: 8″ beaded type with large beaded Silver hub caps.

EQUIPMENT: Motometer, windshield.

FINISH: Body in Hazelwood Brown with Orange trim. Wheels in Orange. Windshield in Hazelwood Brown.

PACKED: One to a carton. WEIGHT: 25 lbs.

Model No. B505

Chrysler Automobile

Model No. B535

(For Children 2 to 5 Years)

SPECIFICATIONS

OVERALL DIMENSIONS: Length, 36″; width, 16″.

WHEELS: 8″ double disc, beaded type, with large silver beaded hub caps and ⅝″ rubber tires.

EQUIPMENT: New type motometer, windshield, bumper, seat pad, and dummy headlights. Has bulb horn.

FENDERS: Front and rear are an integral part of the body.

FINISH: Body in Maroon baked enamel with White trim. Bumper, windshield and steering wheel in Silver. Wheels in White.

PACKING: One to a carton. WEIGHT: 31 lbs.

Special construction reduces set-up work to minimum.

Model No. B5352

This is the same as Model B535 except to be finished in Blue with White trim, wheels in Red. Windshield, bumper and steering wheel in Silver.

Model No. B5353

This is the same as B535 except to be finished in Ivory with Red trim; and wheels, bumpers, steering wheel and windshield in Silver.

Model No. B535

Zephyr De Luxe Automobile

Model No. B573

(For Children 3 to 6 Years)

SPECIFICATIONS

OVERALL DIMENSIONS: Length 42½″; width 17½″.

WHEELS: 10″ ball bearing with 2¾″ white side-walled pneumatic tires.

EQUIPMENT: Complete—French bulb horn, adjustable rubber pedals, radiator ornament, seat pad, Swiss music box radio, new windshield, bumper, hub caps and fender lights. Fenders are part of body.

FINISH: Body in Black baked enamel with Ivory panelling. Wheels in Black. Windshield, bumper, hub caps and fender lights all chromium plated.

PACKED: One in a carton.

SHIPPING WEIGHT: 46 lbs.

Construction reduces dealer's set-up work to a minimum.

Model No. B573

Chrysler Fire Chief Auto

Model No. B536

(For Children 2 to 5 Years)

SPECIFICATIONS

OVERALL DIMENSIONS: Length, 36″; width, 16″.

WHEELS: 8″ double disc, beaded type, with large silver beaded hub caps and ⅝″ rubber tires.

EQUIPMENT: Large chromium plated Fire Chief bell, dummy headlights, seat pad, bumper and new windshield.

FENDERS: Front and rear are an integral part of the body.

FINISH: Body in Red baked enamel with White trim. Wheels in White. Steering wheel, windshield and bumper in Silver.

PACKING: One to a carton. WEIGHT: 31 lbs.

Special construction reduces set-up work to minimum.

Model No. B536

New SPEED-O-MATIC DRIVE

Not this!

CONVENTIONAL CHAIN DRIVE
Round and round foot action wastes knee room. Large part of pedal cycle applies no power. Poor body position for comfort and application of power.

Not this!

CONVENTIONAL DIRECT DRIVE
Gives good body position and foot action but lacks smoothness and power of Speed-O-Matic drive.

This!

⅓ **Easier to pedal**
Back and forth foot action. Ample leg room. Entire thrust of foot applies power. Good body position for comfort, application of power.

2-speed
SPEED-O-MATIC GEAR SHIFT

LOW GEAR provides powerful 1 to 1 ratio for climbing hills, pedaling on rough surfaces. Gear shift lever works just like real car.

HIGH GEAR at 2 to 1 ratio gives twice the speed with no more noticeable effort. Child can readily feel gear change, see speed change.

SHIFTING GEARS can be done standing still or when car is going. Child just coasts for a moment and shifts. Impossible to damage gears.

JET LINER CONVERTIBLE
Speed-O-Matic Chain Drive
MODEL A-521

DIMENSIONS: Length 36", width 19".

SPEED-O-MATIC DRIVE: Combination of pedal and chain type drive, giving advantage of reciprocal motion of pedal drive and geared ratio of chain drive.

BEARINGS: Two ball bearings in rear frame. Oilless bronze bearings in sprocket assembly and on rear axle.

TIRES: 8" x ⅝" solid rubber.

SEAT PAD: Tough fiber. Red.

TRIM: Chrome plated hub caps, hood ornament.

FINISH: Iridescent turquoise body. Ivory steering wheel, windshield, wheels and lettering. Bumpers, grill and headlamps painted silver.

PACKING: One per carton.

SHIPPING WEIGHT: Approx. 34 lbs.

Speed-O-Matic drive

SUPER JET CONVERTIBLE
Two Speed Speed-O-Matic Chain Drive
MODEL A-522

DIMENSIONS: Length 36", width 19".

DRIVE: Two Speed. Shifts from low ratio (1 to 1) to high (2 to 1). Impossible to strip gears. New Speed-O-Matic drive combines best features of push pedal and chain drive. It has the reciprocal action of pedal drive and the geared ratio of chain drive.

GEAR SHIFT: Actually works. Topped with red plastic knob.

TIRES: 8" x ⅝" solid rubber.

BEARINGS: Two ball bearings in rear frame. Oilless bronze bearings in sprocket assembly and on rear axle.

SEAT PAD: Tough fiber. Red.

TRIM: Chrome plated hub caps, hood ornament.

FINISH: Light blue body. White wheels, steering wheel, windshield, lettering. Grill, bumpers and headlamps painted silver.

PACKING: One per carton.

SHIPPING WEIGHT: Approx. 36 lbs.

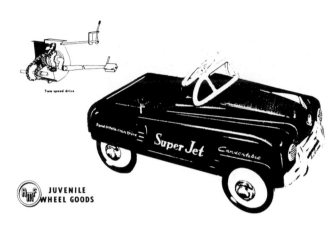

Two speed drive

JUVENILE WHEEL GOODS

Early 1950s AMF

MAINLINER DUMP TRUCK
Pedal Drive   MODEL A-516

DIMENSIONS: Length 41", width 19".

DRIVE: Pedal drive with ball bearings in pull straps and rear frame.

PEDALS: Pedals can be adjusted to three positions.

TIRES: 8" x ⅝" solid rubber.

SEAT PAD: Tough fiber. Black.

DUMP BOX: Large capacity. Easy to operate.

TRIM: Chrome plated hub caps and hood ornament.

FINISH: Yellow body and wheels. Black steering wheel, windshield, dump box, dump handle and side trim. Bumpers and grill painted silver.

PACKING: One per carton.

SHIPPING WEIGHT: Approx. 36 lbs.

Chrome plated hood ornament and hub caps

Dump box with lever

Ball bearings in pedal pull straps and rear frame

Adjustable pedals

MAINLINER HOOK & LADDER
Pedal Drive   MODEL A-518

DIMENSIONS: Length 48", width 19".

DRIVE: Pedal drive with ball bearings in pull straps and rear frame.

PEDALS: Can be adjusted to three positions.

TIRES: 8" x ⅝" solid rubber.

STEP PLATFORM: Has step platform and hand rails.

SEAT PAD: Tough fiber. Black.

TRIM: Chrome plated hub caps and bell.

FINISH: Red body. White steering wheel, windshield, hand rails and wheels. Bumpers, grill, bell hanger and headlamps painted silver. Ladders stained yellow.

PACKING: One per carton.

SHIPPING WEIGHT: Approx. 36 lbs.

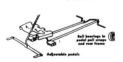

Rear view — step platform and hand rails

JUVENILE WHEEL GOODS

PACESETTER CONVERTIBLE
Pedal Drive   MODEL A-511

DIMENSIONS: Length 36", width 19".

DRIVE: Pedal drive with pull straps that can be adjusted to three positions.

BALL BEARINGS: In pedal pull straps and rear frame.

TIRES: 8" x ¾" solid rubber.

SEAT PAD: Tough fiber. Red.

TRIM: Plated hood ornament and hub caps.

FINISH: Blue body. White wheels, steering wheel, windshield, and stenciling on sides. Bumpers, grill and headlamps are painted silver.

PACKING: One per carton.

SHIPPING WEIGHT: Approx. 31 lbs.

Chrome plated hood ornament

Chrome plated hub caps

Pedal drive

Adjustable pedals

Ball bearings in rear frame and pull straps

Solid rubber tires

Chrome plated bell

MAINLINER FIRE CHIEF
Pedal Drive   MODEL A-513

DIMENSIONS: Length 36", width 19".

DRIVE: Pedal drive with ball bearings in pull straps and rear frame.

PEDALS: Can be adjusted to three positions.

TIRES: 8" x ¾" solid rubber.

SEAT PAD: Tough fiber. Black.

TRIM: Plated hub caps and bell.

FINISH: Red body. White wheels, steering wheel. Bumpers, grill, headlamps and bell hanger painted silver.

PACKING: One per carton.

SHIPPING WEIGHT: Approx. 31 lbs.

AMF JUVENILE WHEEL GOODS

Early 1950s AMF

JET LINER HOOK & LADDER
Speed-O-Matic Chain Drive
MODEL A-528

DIMENSIONS: Length 48", width 19".

SPEED-O-MATIC DRIVE: Combination of pedal and chain type drive, giving advantage of reciprocal motion of pedal drive and geared ratio of chain drive.

BEARINGS: Two ball bearings in rear frame. Oilless bronze bearings in sprocket assembly and on rear axle.

TIRES: 8" x ¾" solid rubber.

REAR STEP: Heavy gauge steel step platform and hand rails.

SEAT PAD: Tough fiber. Black.

TRIM: Chrome plated hub caps, bell. Red, black and silver emblem.

FINISH: Red body. White steering wheel, windshield, wheels. Bumpers, grill, bell hanger and headlamps painted silver. Ladders stained yellow.

PACKING: One per carton.

SHIPPING WEIGHT: Approx. 37 lbs.

Chrome plated bell

Ball bearings in rear frame

Speed-O-Matic Chain Drive

Simulated wire wheels with semi-pneumatic tires

SUPER SPORT CONVERTIBLE
Speed-O-Matic Chain Drive
MODEL A-531

DIMENSIONS: Length 36", width 19".

SPEED-O-MATIC DRIVE: Combination of pedal and chain type drive, giving advantage of reciprocal motion of pedal drive and geared ratio of chain drive.

BEARINGS: Two ball bearings in front wheels and two in rear frame. Oilless bronze bearings in sprocket assembly and on rear axle.

WHEELS: Simulated wire wheels with 7½"x1¼" semi-pneumatic tires.

TRIM: Chrome plated hub caps and headlamps.

FINISH: Iridescent Aztec Gold body. Matador Red seat trim and wheels. Red lettering with black outline. Black steering wheel. Windshield and grill painted silver.

PACKING: One per carton.

SHIPPING WEIGHT: Approx. 34 lbs.

AMF JUVENILE WHEEL GOODS

SPORTLINER STATION WAGON
Speed-O-Matic Chain Drive
MODEL A-534

DIMENSIONS: Length 42½", width 19".

SPEED-O-MATIC DRIVE: Combination of pedal and chain type drive, giving advantage of reciprocal motion of pedal drive and geared ratio of chain drive.

BEARINGS: Two ball bearings in front wheels and two in rear frame. Oilless bronze bearings in sprocket assembly and on rear axle.

WHEELS: Simulated wire wheels with 7½"x1¼" semi-pneumatic tires.

REAR BOX: Large capacity, for carrying toys, etc. Heavy gauge steel hand rails.

TRIM: Chrome plated hub caps and headlamps.

FINISH: Iridescent Jade body. Ivory steering wheel, windshield, hand rails, wheels and trim on sides and seat. Grill painted silver.

PACKING: One per carton.

SHIPPING WEIGHT: Approx. 35 lbs.

SPORTLINER HOOK & LADDER
Speed-O-Matic Chain Drive
MODEL A-538

DIMENSIONS: Length 48", width 19".

SPEED-O-MATIC DRIVE: Combination of pedal and chain type drive giving advantage of reciprocal motion of pedal drive and geared ratio of chain drive.

BEARINGS: Two ball bearings in front wheels and two in rear frame. Oilless bronze bearings in sprocket assembly and on rear axle.

WHEELS: Simulated wire wheels with 7½"x1¼" semi-pneumatic tires.

REAR STEP: Heavy gauge steel step platform and hand rails.

TRIM: Chrome plated hub caps, bell and headlamps. Red, black and silver emblem.

FINISH: Red body. White steering wheel, windshield, wheels, trim on sides and seat. Bell hanger and grill painted silver. Ladders stained yellow. Red, black, yellow and white decals on side.

PACKING: One per carton.

SHIPPING WEIGHT: Approx. 39 lbs.

JUVENILE WHEEL GOODS

Early 1950s AMF

RACER
Speed-O-Matic Chain Drive
MODEL A-550

DIMENSIONS: Length 41", width 19".

SPEED-O-MATIC DRIVE: Combination of pedal and chain type drive giving advantage of reciprocal motion of pedal drive and geared ratio of chain drive.

BEARINGS: Oilless bronze bearings in sprocket assembly and on rear axle. Two ball bearings on rear axle in body.

WHEELS: Semi-pneumatic tires:

Front 8" x 1½"; rear 10" x 1½". Nylon bearings in front wheels.

SHIFTING LEVER: Located on side of car.

FINISH: Yellow body and wheels. Black trim on hood and rear. Black steering wheel, front bar, and shifting lever. Red lettering.

PACKING: One per carton.

SHIPPING WEIGHT: Approx. 34 lbs.

ROAD KING WAGON
MODEL C-435

DIMENSIONS: Box is 35" long, 17" wide, 4½" deep.

CONSTRUCTION: All heavy gauge steel with embossings, for added strength.

TIRES: 10" x 1¾", semi-pneumatic.

BEARINGS: Nylon bearings in all wheels.

HUB CAPS: Painted silver.

FINISH: Red body and wheels. Black handle and frame. White lettering.

PACKING: One per carton.

SHIPPING WEIGHT: Approx. 34 lbs.

JUVENILE WHEEL GOODS

TIE IN WITH ADS LIKE THIS
APPEARING IN SATURDAY EVENING POST

BMC TOYS
CAN TAKE THE
ROUGHEST PUNISHMENT
(EVEN FROM CHILDREN!)

BMC – THE ONLY TOYS WITH KNEE ACTION!
Genuine "AUTO" knee action that actually works!

BMC TOYS GROW UP WITH YOUR CHILDREN!
Designed for children from 3 to 8 years, the wide seats and pedals adjust as your child grows! Above you see the chain drive DeLuxe Tractor with KNEE ACTION and Dump Cart attached; the KNEE Action Sidewalk Bike complete with Trainer Wheels; and the Thunderbolt Station Wagon with sturdy, one piece, realistic body and chrome bell.

YOU CAN'T PLAY WITH A BROKEN TOY!
If there ever was a way to send money down the drain, it's to buy a toy that can't take rough abuse from children! This is where BMC-built toys are at their best. For the solid steel "auto" construction . . . the structural engineering . . . the kind of high quality craftsmanship you just don't associate with toys . . . goes into every BMC unit built!

LIGHTWEIGHT, RUGGED, SAFE!
Most important, BMC toys are safe as they are sound! Your child can't get scratched or cut on the smooth, rolled edges. And to check tipping, BMC toys have a lower center of gravity. The ball-bearing wheels have puncture-proof tires.

AND THE PRICE IS RIGHT!
But as much as kids love BMC toys, grown-ups like the prices! Actually, with the tremendous array of styles and types, there's a BMC toy to fit the tightest budget. The prices range from $9.95 to $35.95 at better department stores and at hardware, toy and bicycle shops. Sometime soon, take your youngster to the BMC Dealer in your neighborhood and get the facts about the educational new BMC Bike and Motor Club. You'll both have the time of your lives!

JET LINER DUMP TRUCK

BLUE STREAK

FREE !

BMC BIKE & MOTOR CLUB

You will be notified in advance of publication dates and will receive pre-prints as well as proofs of suggested tie-in ads, mats of which will be available.

BMC The "Mark" in wheel goods

FEATURES THAT SELL

Cars and tractors with bicycle type chain drive and ball bearings in hangers for easy pedaling. Supported on rigid frames.

Ball bearings in pull straps of all pedal drive cars. Pedals are adjustable.

Automotive type steering for perfect steering control.

Ball bearings in rear axle hangers make tractors and cars easier to operate.

Wide seats with safe rolled edges on all models. Thunderbolt cars feature duo-seat.

Knee action on tractors and bicycle. Tractors have new sturdy front fork.

Ball bearings in bicycle wheel and sprocket assembly. Replaceable.

All BMC tractor seats are adjustable for longer usefulness. BMC bike seats can be raised or lowered to four positions.

BMC's famous Thunderbolt body is all one piece.

Ball bearings in BMC Feather Weight Bicycle sprocket assembly insure easy pedaling. Replaceable.

Ball bearing wheels make models faster, easier to operate.

1953 Advertising Ads

TRACTOR SERIES

TDL
DeLuxe Tractor

TRS
Tractor Sr. Heavy Duty

TRJ-1
Tractor Jr. Heavy Duty

TRJ-2
Tractor Junior

BLUE STREAK SERIES

BLS
Blue Streak

THUNDERBOLT SERIES

SWT
Station Wagon

CT
Convertible

HLT
Hook & Ladder

CHALLENGER SERIES

CDT
Dump Truck

CSW
Station Wagon

CFC
Fire Chief

CHL
Hook & Ladder

JET LINER SERIES

JDT
Dump Truck

JSW
Station Wagon

JC
Convertible

JHL
Hook & Ladder

ATTACHMENTS

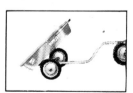

1-A
Dump Cart

2-A
Trailer

3-A
Scoop

4-A
Snow Plow

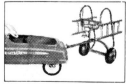

5-A
Fire Fighter

6-A
Grader

SIDEWALK BICYCLES

BS
Sidewalk Bike

COASTER WAGON

RK
Road King

SPECIAL SERIES - RACERS

R-8
Racer

R-2
Racer

WK-35   **Wheel Kit**

WK-33   **Wheel Kit**

TRADE MARKS, EMBLEMS, ETC.

The "Mark" in wheel goods

TRADE MARK

BMC Trademark mats are available in the following widths: 2¾", 2⅛", 1½", 1⅛", ¾". Please specify size.

Coloring Book

BMC Coloring Book of Safety Rules mat is available in 1⅞" width.

BE-EM-CEE

Be-Em-Cee trademark mats are available in the following sizes: 1¾" and 3⅜" high, facing either to the right or left.

KNEE ACTION

Knee Action Logotype mats are available in 1" or 1⅜" widths.

EMBLEM

BMC Bike & Motor Club Emblem mats are available in widths of ⅞" or 1⅞".

These mats are made available to you to help you prepare your ads. Since most of the 1953 BMC line is new, the great majority of the mats you now have are obsolete. We suggest you dispose of them and use these new half-tones. In making up your ads don't forget the Bike & Motor Club merchandising. The FREE Coloring Book of Safety Rules will please parents and children alike, as will the beautiful Bike & Motor Club Emblem and decal and the authentic driver's license.

Check Page one for features that make BMC Wheel Goods the greatest line in America. These show why BMC toys rank with the best. (In ordering mats please use code numbers shown.)

with the purchase of any BMC Wheel Goods—

1. **MEMBERSHIP**
   In BMC's Bike & Motor Club

2. **DRIVER'S LICENSE**

3. **COLORING BOOK OF SAFETY RULES**

4. **CLUB EMBLEM**
   Press on clothing or hat

5. **CLUB DECAL**
   Place on toy

1953 Advertising Ads

43

1953 Advertising Ads

2 TDL
DeLuxe Tractor

2 TRJ-2
Tractor Junior

2 TRS
Tractor Senior
Heavy Duty

2 TRJ-1
Tractor Junior
Heavy Duty

2 JDT
Jet Dump Truck

2 CSW
Challenger
Station Wagon

2 HLT
Thunderbolt
Hook & Ladder

2 BLS
Blue Streak

2 BS
Sidewalk Bike

2 R8
Racer

Hamilton tow truck

No. 808

1958 HAMILTON CATALOG

A realistic type tow truck that every youngster will cherish

Complete with horn and tow truck tool box

The desire of every little mechanic

The towing hoist really works, just like the real tow trucks. Complete in every detail.

The little mechanics will shine with pride when they see the real horn, handsome tool box and a genuine towing hoist, and they all really work. The thrill of actually pushing another car with the large front bumper, hanging on to the side of the two hand rails, will be a thrill that comes only once in a lifetime. Large semi-pneumatic jeep type tires—easiest steering possible—2 seat positions for different age children and the ease of pedal operation will make this an easy seller with the "little mechanics" set.

- **2 SEATS FOR DIFFERENT AGE CHILDREN**
- **TOWING HOIST** • **2 TOW TRUCK TYPE HAND RAILS**
- **LARGE FRONT BUMPER** • **HORN** • **TOOL BOX**
- **1¼" x 8" SEMI PNEUMATIC JEEP TYPE TIRES**

39 lbs. Packed one in a carton 16⅛ x 45 x 20⅛

HAMILTON STEEL PRODUCTS, INC.
1845 WEST 74TH STREET • CHICAGO 36, ILLINOIS

"*Hitch your sales to a star*"

HAMILTON'S ORIGINAL

AIR FORCE JEEP
AND
ARMY JEEP

MODEL NO. 800*
MODEL NO. 800C
MODEL NO. 803C

1958 HAMILTON CATALOG

Still the best seller . . .

Now better than ever before.

✪ New low price.

✪ New luxury wheels with semi-pneumatic tires

✪ New shorter turning radius.

✪ New pre-assembled chassis.

✪ These Jeeps bear authentic Air Force markings in red, white, and blue. They are timely, realistic toys loaded with play value. The Hamilton Air Force Jeep is a proven business builder!

SPECIFICATIONS

Easy assembly
Sturdy, welded steel construction
Ball bearing rear axle, push rods and wheels
Baked enamel, Official Air Force Blue
Realistic markings
Two seat levels, three pedal adjustments
Front and rear bumpers
Large 8" wheels, semi-pneumatic 1¼" tires
Press-on permanent locking hub caps

*Model 803: Same car with Army markings

SHIPPING INFORMATION

Packed one to a carton 16⅛" x 20⅛" x 41¼"
Running gear pre-assembled
Shipping weight: 36 lbs.

**Equipped with Steel Linked Chain Drive

46

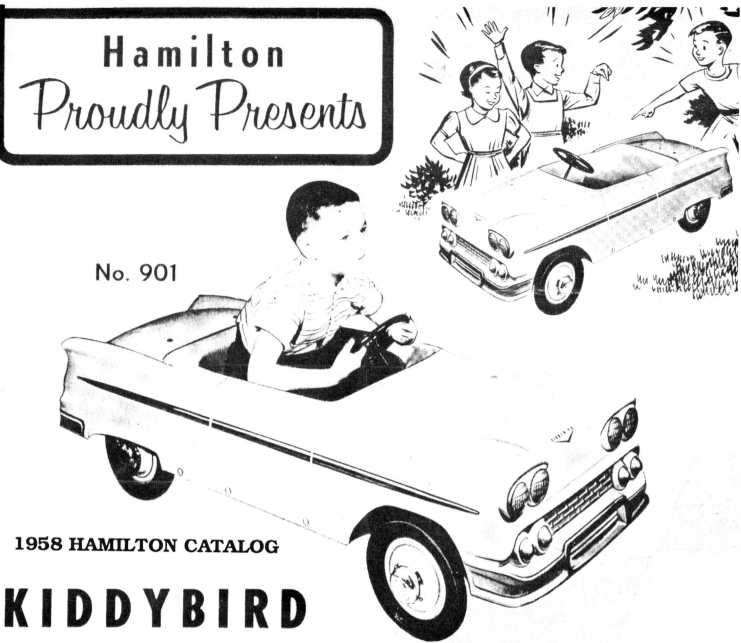

Hamilton Proudly Presents

No. 901

1958 HAMILTON CATALOG

KIDDYBIRD

...the dream of every youngster

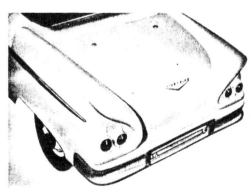

The new 1958 Kiddybird design and style is indeed the dream of every youngster. "Just like dad's new car!" The sculptured all plastic body is securely mounted on a rugged all steel channel constructed frame. Chain drive and easy steering for top performance.

- All plastic body.
- Steel channel constructed frame.
- Wheels 1¼" x 8" semi-pneumatic auto-type tires.
- Chain drive and easy steering.
- 50" long — 21" wide — 43 lbs.

HAMILTON STEEL PRODUCTS, INC.
1845 WEST 74TH STREET • CHICAGO 36, ILLINOIS

47

IRWIN TOYS OF THE 60s
THE FIRST IN THE PLASTIC LINE

The following section was loaned to us from the archives of the Irwin Toy Company. We wish to thank Bertram M. Cohen for so graciously letting us borrow this material. We think this is the first time many of these pages have been printed.

THANKS VERY MUCH TO:

B. M. COHEN
169 MARLBOROUGH ST.
BOSTON, MA 02116

THE EDITOR

TOY & HOBBY WORLD

Volume 8, Number 5   *ERVING THE MASS MERCHANDISING TOY & HOBBY MARKET*   March 2, 1970

IRWIN CORP. A PIONEER IN NEW TOY MATERIALS

NASHUA, N. H. — The "fac .." of today's plastics-dominated toy industry may well be Irwin Cohn, sident and chairman of the board of the Irwin Corporation.

A co-founder of the Irwin Corp ment and use of innovative plastic was founded in 1922.

Irwin Cohn

Cohn's and Irwin's combined histories are replete with "firsts." He introduced the blowing method of producing toys to the industry in 1922. It is said that he also was responsible for the first injection molded toys; tube blow-molded toys; styrene blow molded toys; acetate blow molded toys and polyethylene blow molded toys.

Irwin Corp. introduced polyethylene injection molded toys in the shape of cars and trucks, to equal their steel counterparts in strength and play value. The company was also the first to spray color on acetate toys and to employ vacuum metallizing on toys.

Uniquely, Irwin Corp. also makes its own plastic raw materials, which are used not only in toys, but in automobiles, houses, shoes, garden hose, wire covering, floor tile, rainwear and other articles.

In its first years as a toy manufacturer, Irwin Corp. made celluloid baby rattles and celluloid pinwheels. Its sale of these items was so great, in fact, that the company came to be known as the "pinwheel and rattle king."

During World War II, when plastic and metal materials were on allocation, Cohn's ingenuity resulted in the development of plastic ma-

Cohn has spearheaded the development materials and toys since the company

with producers of polyethylene with a view towards developing a product to surmount the shortcomings of styrene and earlier plastic materials, which proved to be extremely brittle and in some cases unsafe.

"We tried to convince the trade that this was the toy of the future, that it wouldn't break like styrene," Cohn recalled at a recent interview. "At Toy Fair we threw the toy around our showroom to demonstrate its strength."

There was some initial opposition to the new material, but this soon dissipated and the item became a great sales success.

According to Mr. Cohn, the new materials developed by Irwin were conceived largely out of "necessity" and to "combat fears" of mothers about the properties of other materials.

In 1945 at the recommendation of a major account, Irwin gave up celluloid because of the fire hazard involved in products made of this material. The company turned instead to developing for toy use such other materials as acetate and butyrate. This was followed by styrene and then polyethylene as basic raw materials for toys.

By 1960 Irwin was making a plastic blow-molded racing car 54" long, which was the largest blown plastic item of that time. During Toy Fair that year. Irwin salesmen rode the car up and down the halls of 200 Fifth Avenue to show that it, too, was durable and practical.

A major hit item for the company was a plastic sports car for Barbie and Ken, made in 1962 under license by Mattel. Some $2.5 million worth of this item was sold in its first year of marketing.

According to Mr. Cohn, Irwin made the industry's first plastic tea sets of celluloid in the 1920's. It made the first chain drive plastic bicycle under license from Honda Corp., and developed plastic swings into a large business four to five years ago.

Irwin's first concern has always been for the safety and welfare of the child who will use and enjoy the toys. Historically, the company has evaluated materials and designs with a view toward eliminating any and all hazards in the use of its toys.

"Vesta" motorscooter with enclosed chain drive. chrome handlebars, heavy duty rubber tires on steel wheels, was innovative 1962 item.

The guiding hand behind these and other pioneering developments has been Mr. Cohn. who largely originates the ideas for new toy designs put into effect by the company. The ideas are carried out by designers and technicians connected with Irwin and its affiliated firms.

Irwin Cohn is a complex individual. He set out to master the intricacies of the plastics business, and

has been eminently successful in reaching his goals. He disclaims any skills as an engineer or designer, yet through the years he has demonstrated an uncanny ability to make machines work for him when they did not for others, and to perfect designs that even the most accomplished developers could not bring to a practical, workable conclusion.

With its past history of innovations, the Irwin Corporation has surprisingly remained content with its strong, still-growing place among toy manufacturers.

"My cup of tea has been to develop items," Cohn commented. "My interest ends when the item is ready for market. I am not good at selling. But I've been pretty much content with what I have."

Nevertheless, Irwin Corporation is an expanding company, and has more than doubled its business in the past few years. In 1969 it registered a 25-30% increase in sales over the previous year.

Today Irwin Corporation has one of the most complete, self-sustaining vertical toy manufacturing operations in the world. Employing some 800 persons, the company is engaged in all processes of production, from the making of plastic raw materials to the manufacture of finished toys.

The company has its own tool and die manufacturing shop, and its own foundry to cast blowing dies. Irwin does its own silver plating, coloring and spraying, and has its own model shop and printing shop.

In its manufacturing complex at Nashua, N.H., the company stores an inventory of toy dies and molds worth some $20 million, ranging in size from dies for small plastic toys, to dies for such large ones as the racing car.

A year ago Irwin acquired the use of all the tools and dies of the Andy Gard Corporation. This enabled Irwin Corp. to provide a steady supply of toys, even during this critical period.

Irwin Corp. made the toy industry's first plastic mechanical toys— crawling dolls, dancing dolls, motor boats, etc. These items sold from 29¢ to $1.98 at retail. The company also produced the first plastic pedal cars, chain drive bicycles, golf sets, bowling sets, bats and balls and many other items. In fact, Irwin has been issued over 100 patents for toy items.

The toy industry's first polyethylene toy, a 7" plastic car, was introduced by the Irwin Corporation in the late 1940's.

BIKES LIKE THE REAL ONES

IN SIT DOWN AND RIDE TOYS

PEDAL ACTION HONDA

A REMARKABLE LIKENESS TO THE WORLD'S FASTEST SELLING MOTORCYCLE

LICENSED BY HONDA

- ONE PIECE CONSTRUCTION
- REMOVABLE TRAINING WHEELS
- MADE OF SUPER STRONG
- IRVILON "777"

- Steel Axles
- Hand Grips
- Attractively Decorated

BEAK OPENS FOR STORAGE

BOTH A PROVEN SUCCESS

A PRODUCT OF IRWIN CORP

NO 5477 OFFICIAL PEDAL HONDA
45" L X 28" H X 16 1/2" W
Equipped with chain drive. As easy to ride as a plain bicycle. Semi Pneumatic tires. Authentic cream and blue. Each boxed - KD

PK 1 EA   WT 22 LBS

NO. 5501 "PELICAN" SIT DOWN AND RIDE.
21" L x 15" H x 9" W.
Beak opens for storage of toys or other articles. Picture label box. Steel axles. Gaily decorated.
Pk. 1/3 dz.   Wgt. 16 lbs.
D– Patent Pending

Hours of fun and rugged Animal Ride 'Ems. Colorful, well designed pieces will take punishment from the most active youngsters. Made of Irvilon "777" with wheels that won't mar the floors.

PEDAL ACTION

NO. 5462 PEDAL MOTORCYCLE
32" L X 13" W X 20" H
Super tough construction. Metal fork brackets, cranks and axles; converts to 2 wheel bicycle. Each boxed - KD.

PK 1 EA . . . . WT 11 1/2 LBS   15

NO. 5500 "WATERMELON" SIT DOWN AND RIDE.
20" L x 6½" W x 10" H.
Funny face watermelon with movable eyes. Steel axles. Gaily decorated.
Pk. ½ dz.   Wgt. 16 lbs.
D – Patent Pending

- STEEL AXLES
- MOVABLE EYES
- HAND GRIP

3

IRWIN CORP. • 200 5th AVENUE • NEW YORK, N.Y.

#5672 - Sit Down & Ride Flipper Toy
(T.M. Lic. Mattel, Inc.
28"L x 12"H gaily decorated Flipper in brite-green w/yellow jumbo wheels & red handlebar.
Pack - 1/2 Dz...... Wt. 21 Lbs.

#4782   BASIC CAR

38″ long, rich, lustrous blue with silver, white and red detail. Adjustable ball-bearing pedal drive. Extra detail molded into body.

Pack 1, weight 16 lbs.

#5421 - PEDAL TRACTOR
26″L x 21″W x 21″H. In brite orange w/chrome-like trim. Steel axles and fork. Super tough construction. Comes w/horn and and trailer hitch.
Pack-1 each....... Wt. - 14 Lbs.

#4719   PEDAL TRACTOR

Bright orange, silver and black. Big 11½″ rear wheels with heavy tractor tread. Working press-down horn. Adjustable seat. Colorful, detailed molded body. Big 26½″x21″x21″.

Pack 1, weight 14 lbs.

IRWIN CORP. • 200 5th AVENUE • NEW YORK, N.Y.

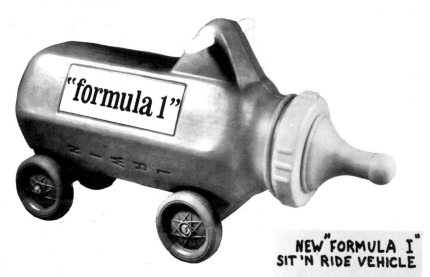

"formula 1"

NEW "FORMULA I" SIT 'N RIDE VEHICLE

5539
Pk. ½ dz.
wt. 13½ lbs.
Bulk Pk.
Ea. assembled
24 x 8½ x 12½

5539 - Sit Down & Ride Bottle
Cap is removable on the front of
bottle. This provides unique
storage of toys, etc. This realistic, Sit 'N Ride toy gives
months of "Learn & Fun Experience".

irwin

CHAIN DRIVE SERPENT

5577 CHAIN DRIVE SERPENT
45'' L x 22'' H x 17'' W
Seat height 12''
Coiled Serpent body and movable head.
Steerable chopper front style front fork.
Strong stability and easy pedaling. All
steel adjustable link chain, gears and
axles. Simulated mag wheels. Silver
decorated features.
Each in 4 color label box.
Pk.: 1 ea..   Wgt.: 20 lbs.

irwin PEDALS TOYS

5564 Chain Drive Indy "500" Racer
Easy pedaling Chain Drive Power. Positive Tru-Action Steering. Silver sprayed details. Simulated Mag wheels. Made of Super Tough Irvilon "777". One piece body construction. A favorite in any competition. Fast—Safe—Built to Race. Orange body and white wind spoiler. Each in full color label box.
Size: 43" l. x 22½" w. x 16" h.
Pack: 1 Each—Wt. 23 lbs.

5560—Chain Drive Chopper
Front wheel 9½" x 2¾". Handsome Chartreuse molded body has authentically detailed "Motor" and high back chopper seat and twin exhaust stacks. Low center of gravity seat gives additional stability and easy pedaling. All steel link chain, gears and axles. Big features include 11½" x 5" wide over-sized rear slicks with simulated mag wheels for easy traction, and stability. Silver decorated features. Each in 4 color label box.
Size: 42½" l. x 29" h. x 18" w.
Pack: 1 Each—Wt. 20 lbs.

5502—Pedal Dune Duggy
Beautifully detailed, highly styled "Mod" Vehicle. New Engineering provides positive easy pedaling. Solid molded Chartreuse body of Irvilon "888". Heavy duty oversized front and rear Mag Wheels. In 2 color White Box.
Size: 38" l. x 20" w. x 16½" h.
Pack: 1 Each—Wt. 16 lbs.

#5498 SHOE – Sit Down & Ride White with gay decorations. L–22" W–8" H 14" approx. Pack ½ doz. Wt. 23 lbs.

54

FUNNY WHEELS

NEW

- STEEL AXLES
- STURDY HAND GRIPS
- DECORATED DETAILS
- MADE OF SUPER TOUGH IRVILON "777"

NEW

NO. 5535 PEANUT SIT
DOWN & RIDE
21"L X 8"W X 14 1/2"H
Looks like the real thing. Colorful ride 'ems
that will draw attention anywhere. Wheels
will not mar floor. Completely assembled.

PK 2 DZ . . . . WT 19 LBS

HUNTS KETCHUP
WITH OFFICIAL LABELS

HUNT'S is a registered trademark
of Hunt–Wesson Foods, Inc.

NO. 5536 OFFICIAL HUNT'S CATSUP SIT
DOWN & RIDE
22"L X 7 3/4"W X 13 1/2"H
Looks like the real thing. Colorful ride 'ems
that will draw attention anywhere. Wheels
will not mar floor. Completely assembled.

PK 1/2 DZ . . . . WT 19 LBS

- MADE OF SUPER TOUGH IRVILON "777"
- OFFICIAL LABELS
- DECORATED DETAILS
- STEEL AXLES
- STURDY HAND GRIPS

OFFICIAL CABANA BANANA

NEW

NO. 5534 OFFICIAL CABANA BANANA SIT
DOWN & RIDE
23"L X 7 3/4"W X 14"H
Looks like the real thing. Colorful ride 'ems
that will draw attention anywhere. Wheels
will not mar floor. Completely assembled.

CABANA® USED BY PERMISSION OF © 1969 STANDARD FRUIT

PK 1/2 DZ . . . . WT 19 LBS

WHEEL GOODS

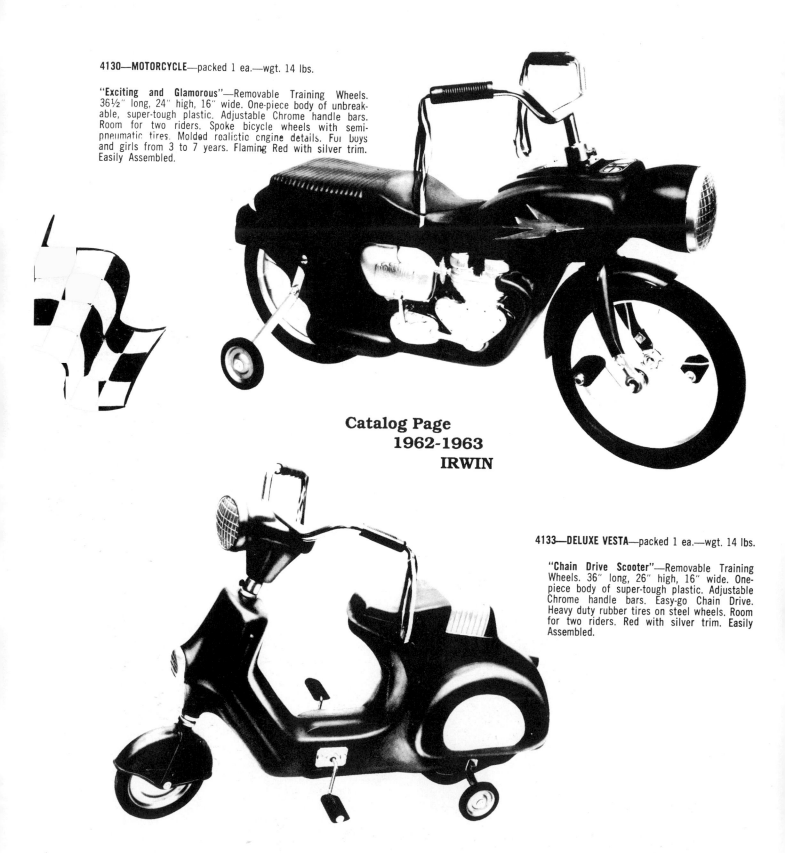

4130—MOTORCYCLE—packed 1 ea.—wgt. 14 lbs.

"Exciting and Glamorous"—Removable Training Wheels. 36½" long, 24" high, 16" wide. One-piece body of unbreakable, super-tough plastic. Adjustable Chrome handle bars. Room for two riders. Spoke bicycle wheels with semi-pneumatic tires. Molded realistic engine details. For boys and girls from 3 to 7 years. Flaming Red with silver trim. Easily Assembled.

**Catalog Page
1962-1963
IRWIN**

4133—DELUXE VESTA—packed 1 ea.—wgt. 14 lbs.

"Chain Drive Scooter"—Removable Training Wheels. 36" long, 26" high, 16" wide. One-piece body of super-tough plastic. Adjustable Chrome handle bars. Easy-go Chain Drive. Heavy duty rubber tires on steel wheels. Room for two riders. Red with silver trim. Easily Assembled.

PEDAL TRACTOR

4719—PEDAL TRACTOR—packed 1 ea.—wgt. 14 lbs.

"Will Really Take the Hard Use"—Molded in durable Plastic. Steel Axles — Ball Bearings — Steel Forks and Supporting Brackets. Rubber Tread on front wheel for Positive Gripping Action. Trailer Hook-up provided. Simulated side view of Engine and Grill. Grooved Pedals. Easily Assembled. Size: 27" x 21" x 20"

**Catalog Page
1962 -1963
IRWIN**

Deluxe FIRE ENGINE

4723—DELUXE FIRE ENGINE—packed 1 ea.—wgt. 19 lbs.

"A Youngster's Delight"—38" long, 17" wide, 17½" high. One-piece body of super tough plastic. Heavy duty pedal mechanism. Rubber tires on steel wheels. Gong bell and rope. Blazing red with black steering wheel and silver trim. Much sculptured detail. Two Wood Ladders on Steel Brackets. Easily Assembled.

1962-63 *Line*

by IRWIN

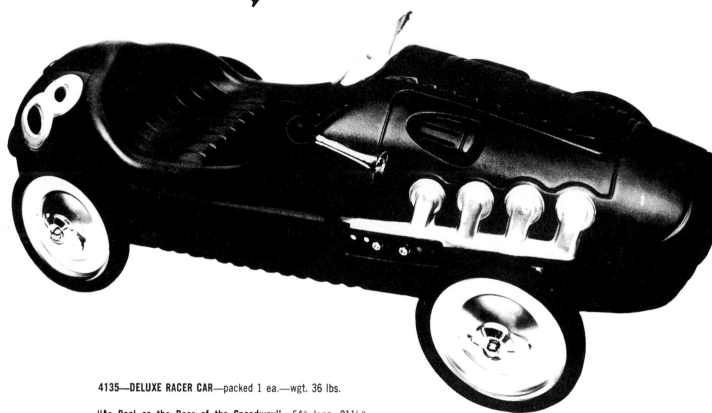

4135—DELUXE RACER CAR—packed 1 ea.—wgt. 36 lbs.

"As Real as the Roar of the Speedway"—54" long, 21½" high, 25½" wide. One piece body of unbreakable, super-tough Irvilon "777". Chain drive, 11¾" ball bearing wheels. Racing type Hub Caps. Heavy duty rubber tires on steel wheels. Extra large legroom space. So light a 3 year old can pedal with ease, so big a 9 year old fits in easily. Bright red with silver trim. Easily assembled. Loud horn.

4134—RACER CAR—packed 1 ea.—wgt. 36 lbs.

Same as the #4135 but without the Horn, Racing Type Hub Caps and Silver Trim.

4127—HORSE AND SULKY—packed 1 ea.—wgt. 11 lbs.

"Toy of Action"—34" long, 19¾" high, 12½" wide. Tough, lightweight plastic horse. Realistic decoration. Sturdy steel pedal mechanism. Heavy duty rubber tires on steel wheels. Contoured plastic seat. Easily Assembled.

58

#4783 FIRE CHIEF

38″ long. Flaming red with white and silver. Authentic fire chief details inc. chrome bell. Adjustable ball-bearing drive.

Pack 1, weight 16½ lbs.

#4784 STATION WAGON

Brilliant green with silver, white and red detail. Authentic wood grain colored side panels. 38″ long. Travel stickers. Safety belt. Plated horn and play gear shift. Adjustable ball-bearing pedal drive.

Pack 1, weight 16 1/2 lbs.

#4785 POLICE CAR

Lustrous ''go-green'' with silver, white and red detail. Accessories include siren, flashing light, safety belt. 38″ long. Adjustable ball-bearing pedal drive.

Pack 1, weight 16½ lbs.

#4786 SPORTS CAR

Rich, brilliant green with authentic racing car detail including twin exhaust stacks (both sides). Has safeth belts, gear shift, plated horn. A jazzy special with silver, red and white stripes, meet stickers, numbers, etc. 38″ long.

Pack 1, weight 17 lbs.

#4787 FIRE TRUCK

Bold bright red, big 43″ truck with ladders, handholds and rear stop plate. Has flashing light and chrome bell. Silver, white and black detail. Play value plus.

Pack 1, weight 18 lbs.

Ride-ems for younger set that represent ▶ • **BIG VALUE** • *UNIQUE DESIGN* • *LASTING QUALITY*

#4788   PEDAL BULLDOZER

Orange, blue and silver with white, red and black detail. Rubber tires on steel wheels. 22" long.

Pack 1, weight 5 1/2 lbs.

#4789   CORVETTE

Red with silver, red and white detail. Authentic sports car look. Steel steering column and support braces. 30" long and low, low priced.

Pack 1, weight 7 lbs.

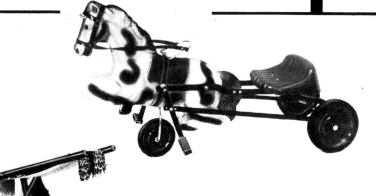

#4127   HORSE and SULKY

Safety, speed and maneuverability in this fine toy now drastically reduced in price. A big value staple. 34" long. Sturdy molded body and seat with steel pedal mechanism and rubber tired wheels. Red, white and black.

Pack 1, weight 11 lbs.

#4176   FLINTSTONES PEDAL CAR w/CANOPY

Ride the TV tie-in for profitable volume sales. 44" long. Molded Flintstane detail throughout. A unique pedal drive.

Pack 1, weight 26 lbs.

#4715   As above, without canopy.
Pack 1, weight 24 lbs.

SUPERMAN

NEW

OVER 2½ FEET LONG

No. 5455 SUPERMAN® PEDAL CAR
37" L x 16" x 19" H. Light weight — Rust resistant. Steel wheels w/rubber tires. Lite Blue w/Silver Trim and Superman Decals.
Pk. 1 each. Wt. 18 lbs.
Over 2½ feet long.

NO. 2360 SUPERMAN® HORN
Brite red w/Superman Decal over 2½' Long. Each w/ Superman cardwrap. Pk. 2 dz. Wt. 12 lbs.

BLOW LIKE A BUGLE

SUPERMAN HORN

NEW

© NATIONAL PERIODICAL PUBLICATIONS, INC., 1966

18

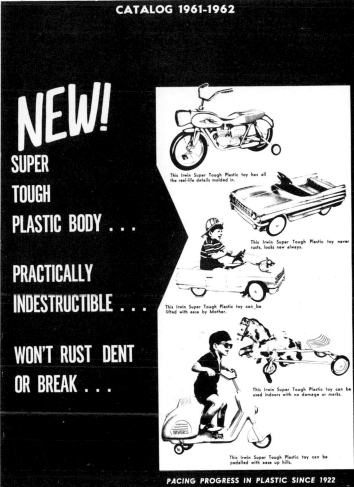

CATALOG 1961-1962

NEW!

SUPER TOUGH PLASTIC BODY . . .

PRACTICALLY INDESTRUCTIBLE . . .

WON'T RUST DENT OR BREAK . . .

This Irwin Super Tough Plastic toy has all the real-life details molded in.

This Irwin Super Tough Plastic toy never rusts, looks new always.

This Irwin Super Tough Plastic toy can be lifted with ease by Mother.

This Irwin Super Tough Plastic toy can be used indoors with no damage or marks.

This Irwin Super Tough Plastic toy can be pedalled with ease up hills.

PACING PROGRESS IN PLASTIC SINCE 1922

IRWIN'S NEW | **BLAZE PEDAL HORSE**

Away out west he'll go on this bronc, so real you'll want to feed him sugar. Made of new, super-tough, extra lightweight plastic that won't rust, dent or break. Double enjoyment value of a play horse and a tricycle.

#4126
• 22½ inches high, 22 inches long, 11½ inches wide.
• White horse with brown spotting.
• Red decorative saddle and detail.
• Rubber tires on red steel wheels.
• Packed 1 per ctn., wt. 6 lbs.
• Easily assembled.

EXCITINGLY NEW

A REAL "HEP" DUNE BUGGY

PEDAL ACTION

• STEERABLE
• NON MAR WHEELS
• DECORATED DETAILS
• STEEL REINFORCED PARTS

NO. 5532 PEDAL DUNE BUGGY
38"L X 20"W X 16 1/4"H
ALL NEW! The latest in styling and detail. Handsomely trimmed. Tru-action steering. Large non mar wheels. Steel axles and reinforced parts. Made of steel strong Irvilon "777". Each boxed - KD.

SUPER-PEDAL WHEEL TOYS

NEW

Honda

PEDAL MINI TRAIL   LICENSED BY HONDA

- STEERABLE
- REMOVABLE TRAINING WHEELS
- PEDAL ACTION
- SPRAYED DETAILS
- ONE PIECE BODY CONSTRUCTION
- STRONG STEEL PARTS

A PRODUCT OF IRWIN CORP
A REMARKABLE LIKENESS TO THE WORLD'S FASTEST SELLING MOTORCYCLE

NO. 5524 OFFICIAL HONDA PEDAL MINI TRAIL
30 1/2" L X 11 1/2" W X 22 1/2" H
Licensed by Honda
A remarkable likeness to the world's fastest selling motorcycle. Two molded 9 1/2" diam. wheels. Each boxed K.D.

PK 1 DZ . . . . WT 9 LBS

13

THE "IN" THING

THE NEW MEAN MACHINE

PEDAL ACTION

NO 5526 MEAN MACHINE
33 L X 13 3 4 W X 25 H
Super tough construction large non mar wheels
Steel axles and reinforced parts made of steel
strong Irvilon 777. Each boxed K.D.

PK 1 EA   WT 8 LBS

- STEERABLE
- STEEL AXLES
- NON MAR WHEELS
- DECORATED DETAILS

PACING PROGRESS IN PLASTIC SINCE 1922

IRWIN'S NEW **SPECIAL RACER CAR**

Almost as real as the roar at the Indianapolis Speedway. We have achieved the ultimate in capturing the imagination of a youngster and building it into this fabulous new Racer Car. Every last detail so important to a boy's heart is molded into the super tough, extra lightweight plastic body that will not rust, dent or break.

#4134
- 54 inches long, 21½ inches high, 25½ inches wide.
- One piece body of unbreakable, super tough Irvilon "777".
- Chain drive, 11¾ inch ball bearing wheels.
- Semi-pneumatic tires on steel wheels.
- Extra large legroom space.
- So light a 3 year old can pedal with ease, so big a 9 year old fits in easily.
- Bright red with silver and black trim.
- Packed 1 per ctn., wt. 36 lbs.
- Easily assembled.

#4135 Deluxe Racer Car
- Same as #4134 but with horn and racing type hub caps.
- Easily assembled.

PACING PROGRESS IN PLASTIC SINCE 1922

IRWIN'S NEW **CONTINENTAL CHAIN DRIVE SCOOTER**

They'll be cutting Continental capers in this ingeniously designed version of that famous Italian scooter. They'll climb the steepest hills with all the ease of a motor but they'll actually be pedaling with the easy-go chain drive. The body is made of extra lightweight super tough plastic that won't rust, dent or break. A real bonus buy with the removable training wheels.

#4132
- **Removable training wheels convert scooter into a regular two wheeler bike.**
- 36 inches long, 26 inches high, 16 inches wide.
- One piece body of super tough plastic.
- Chrome handle-bars, adjustable for height.
- Easy-go chain drive.
- Heavy duty rubber tires on steel wheels.
- Seats two children comfortably.
- Fully sculptured detail molded in for permanence.
- Blue with silver trim.
- Packed 1 per ctn., wt. 14 lbs.
- Easily assembled.

ROADMASTER 1983

G-501
Command Car

This true-to-life Army vehicle is sure to demand attention.

- Rugged, all-steel body with Army Green finish, accented with white army graphics
- Nylon bearing pedal drive adjusts to three positions; delivers power to the 7" x 5/8" molded rubber tires
- Tough, weather-resistant seat pad
- Length 34", width 15"
- Ages two to five

G-500
Rebel Car

Styled to attract young drivers.

- Rugged, all-steel body has a bright Rebel Orange finish with an embossed grille, simulated headlights and a silver bumper
- Racy "11" on the hood and bold Rebel graphics on the side
- Nylon bearing pedal drive adjusts to three positions; delivers power to the 7" x 5/8" molded rubber tires
- Tough, weather-resistant seat pad
- Length 34", width 15"
- Ages two to five

G-480
Trac Mate Wagon

Hitches to any Roadmaster chain-drive tractor to add more play value.

- Heavy-gauge steel body with fully curled Playsafe edges; bright Really Red finish with yellow trim
- Channeled black wagon tongue for strength
- 7" x 3-1/2" cleated tires for easy towing

G-438
Power Pull Tractor

Contemporary design constructed from steel and hi-impact plastic for durability and safety.

- Completely enclosed, nylon bearing chain drive mechanism powers the large, heavy-duty 16" x 4" tractor-tread rear tires
- Recessed grille and headlight decal; eye-catching, four-color engine decals
- Adjustable scoop seat with backrest adds comfort
- Handy trailer hitch fits Trac Mate Wagons
- Wide-stance, 8" x 1-3/4" dual front tires for better stability and an authentic look
- Front suspension "floats" to keep both tires flat, even on an incline
- Ages three to seven

ROADMASTER 1983

G-436 Turbo Trac
- Constructed of durable steel and hi-impact plastic for safety
- Completely enclosed, nylon bearing chain-drive mechanism powers the heavy-duty 10" x 2-3/4" tractor-tread rear tires; 8" x 1-3/4" molded front tires
- Front suspension "floats" to keep both rear tires flat, even on an incline
- Adjustable scoop seat; handy trailer hitch fits Trac Mate Wagons
- Ages three to seven

G-482 Trac Mate Wagon
- Same features as G-480

G-402
Ranch Trac Tractor

Realistic look that lands many young admirers.
- Constructed of durable steel and hi-impact plastic for safety
- Completely enclosed, nylon bearing chain-drive mechanism powers the heavy-duty 10" x 2-3/4" tractor-tread rear tires; 8" x 1-3/4" molded front tire
- Recessed grille and headlight decal; "diesel" hood decal; eye-catching, four-color engine decals
- Adjustable scoop seat; handy trailer hitch fits Trac Mate Wagons
- Ages three to seven

MODERN MIND MULTIPLIES MODELS IN MODEL MEET — When an international model speedboat race was held in a London Park recently, Eric Daniel, one of the British entrants, went in for the model theme in a big way. In a model, modest and careful way, he drove to the model meet in his modern model motor, which towed a model trailer, on which rested his model motorboat. By the way, Eric is a model boy!

Multiply your money by investing in a model manner.

We'll gladly help you with your money matters.

TWO PIECE NEWS PHOTO POSTER FROM 1930s   14 1/2" X 20"

Body by Stalker

No. 7548 PACKARD SIX

Length Overall—51-inches.
Finish—Ottawa tan, with red panel and red and white striping.
Wheels—12 x 1-inch rubber tired-roller bearing disc, finished red.
Gear—Adjustable pedals. Easily propelled. Full Spring Chassis.
Packing—One in crate. Weight—130 lbs.
Equipment—Composition tilting steering wheel. Gas and spark control. Signal horn. Nickeled one piece wind shield with side wings. Rear vision mirror. Spot light. Motor meter. Nickel plated radiator. Metal road lamps with glass lens. License tag. Instrument board. Gear shift. Upholstered seat. Rear hood. Trunk. Two bar bumper. Side door. Heavy die-formed fenders. Kick plates. Rubber pedals. Alemite system, with can of grease. Tool bag with tools. Front and rear springs. Motor buzzer. Stop and go signal. Speedometer.

Side view showing streamline body and rolled edge fenders.

A DISTINCTIVE AND EXCLUSIVE AMERICAN FEATURE

ALEMITE

HIGH PRESSURE LUBRICATING SYSTEM

For American Juvenile Automobiles

THE ONLY JUVENILE AUTO LINE EQUIPPED WITH THIS POWERFUL SALES FEATURE. SHOW THE CHILD AN AUTO EQUIPPED LIKE DAD'S AND THE SALE IS YOURS. AMERICAN AUTOS ALWAYS HAVE THE LATEST.

Motor Meters that are distinctive in design and workmanship.

Oil Can—This feature, distinctively American, is carried under the hood on a special spring carrier fastened to the cowl board. A bottle of the celebrated 3 in 1 oil comes as part of this equipment. Originated by us and not offered by others.

Juvenile Tool Kit with Tools—A distinctive American feature. This was first offered by us.

All Steel Radiators.—American autos are equipped with several attractive all steel designed radiators. The above illustrations show two popular designs equipped with winged motor meter and name plates that are miniature reproductions of name plates on gas propelled autos. We were the first to equip Juvenile Autos with steel radiators.

1925 AMERICAN NATIONAL

DISTINCTIVE AMERICAN FEATURES

MALLEABLE STEERING WHEEL

Invented by us in 1922, and was a big improvement over every type of malleable steering wheel ever put on the market.

COMPOSITION TILTING STEERING WHEEL

An exact reproduction of the large tilting type composition wheel. Perfectly safe when locked and can be tilted to meet the convenience of the driver by releasing button on steering post. Comes equipped with nickel-plated gas and spark control

RUBBER PEDALS

The leading, original and distinctive feature introduced by us in 1923. Still popular as ever on American autos.

FRENCH HORN

SIGNAL HORN

Two new large improved auto horns—plenty of noise. Distinctive and attractive design, found only on American autos.

Improved type hexagon metal road lamps with non-glare glass lens, cross bar and license tags. This distinctive American feature adds much to the attractiveness of American autos.

INSTRUMENT BOARD

The most attractive and complete instrument board ever introduced. This high grade feature has rich satin bronze finish. Latest design instrument dials. Adjustable clock hands. Realistic operating speedometer which registers when auto is in action. Ignition switch operates Motor Buzzer "On" and "Off."

ADDITIONAL AMERICAN PATENTED FEATURES

Gas and Spark Control
Patented March 5th, 1924.
One-piece Windshield with Side Wings and Spot Light
Patented March 5th, 1924.
All Steel Seat
Patented May 26th, 1924.
Stop and Go Signal
Patented November 25th, 1924.

Cantelever Springs and Axle Bearings
Patented March 5th, 1924.
Double Disc Steel Wheel
Patented April 7th, 1924.
Hub Caps
Patented March 5th, 1924.

AMERICAN IMPROVED AUTO GEAR

Adjustable Pedals
Easy Running

Long, Powerful Pedal Stroke
High Geared

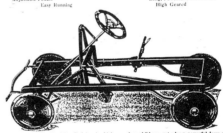

NOTE—Extra long stroke of pedals. Pedals raise high enough so child can get a long, powerful down stroke.

In this new improved Auto Gear we have a gear that should appeal to every Juvenile Auto buyer. The long, powerful pedal stroke enables the child to get more speed and pleasure with less effort.

The adjustable pedals make it possible to adjust the gear to fit the child, thereby greatly adding to the efficiency of the auto and satisfaction of the child. See catalog description for autos taking this gear.

MOTOR BUZZER

(Patented March 5th, 1925)
Going into its Fourth Successful Season

The Motor Noise Maker. The feature that gives the child the thrill of motoring. Ignition switch operates Motor Buzzer "on" and "off." This wonderfully designed piece of mechanism reproduces a very correct imitation of a motor in action. Just like all other "American" features it makes its special appeal to the kiddies. Just imagine the enthusiasm they will show when they see an auto "Just like Dad's" with every sound of a sweet, soft running motor.

THE GREATEST GIFT
Your Boy Can Have

Whether he is 4 or 14 he will get the greatest thrill of his life, satisfy his craving for speed, with safety, and be ready at all times to do your shopping for you, if Christmas brings him a

SAMSON KAR

This car, operated by hand, will not tire the four-year-old; sliding seat adjusts to size for older boys up to 13 or 14. Develops every muscle in the body, runs so easily a small girl can operate it, and is built to last. Guaranteed for a year and will stand the racket for many years.

Seat is only $8\frac{1}{2}$ inches from ground, so "spills" cause no injury. Single disc wheels of steel, 12 inches high prevent tipping. Tires $1\frac{1}{2}$ inches diameter. Seat, handle and bottom of tray of wood—all the rest steel and iron.

Indestructible, but beautiful. Wheels are painted red, the rest of the car blue.

COMFORT, SPEED STRENGTH, SAFETY

All the children can use it as it is so easy to adjust to required size. Gives added strength to arms, lungs, legs and back. As easy to stop as to start. No over-exertion possible.

Buy from your department, toy or hardware store. Show them this advertisement. If they cannot supply, order direct, sending $15.00. We will send all charges paid. Sent C. O. D., if you prefer.

SAMSON MANUFACTURING CO.
310 Cliff Street   **Springfield, Ohio**

BMC TOYS
GIVE CHILDREN
KNEE ACTION
(and lots of it!)

BMC's are the world's only toys with genuine "auto" KNEE ACTION that actually works.

Shown above are the new chain drive DeLuxe Tractor with Knee Action and dump cart attached; the sidewalk bike, with Trainer Wheels has a real Knee Action shock absorber for a smooth, jolt-free ride. Challenger Fire Chief has push pedals adjustable to three positions...ages 3 to 8.

Stop building a toy junk pile!

BMC toys are built to stand up to the knocks and bangs roughest drivers give them. Structural engineering plus sturdy steel "auto" construction go into every BMC toy. Especially designed for children from ages 3 to 8 ... the seats and pedals adjust with your child's growth.

Designed for safety-first!

Your child can't get cut or scratched on the smooth, rolled edges of every BMC toy. Like the new sports cars,

BMC toys have a lower center of gravity to check tipping. The ball bearing wheels have puncture proof tires.

Prices to fit tightest budget!

BMC toys start as low as $9.95, and range to $34.95, at better department stores and at hardware, toy and bicycle shops. See the BMC Dealer in your neighborhood soon. Turn your youngster loose and let him "test drive" any one of the numerous styles and types. You'll find BMC toys are irresistible to oldsters and small fry alike. The fun is built right in!

Chain Drive 'Jetliner' Dump Truck   Pedal Drive 'Blue Streak'

FREE!
Children's Coloring Book of Safety Rules for your Youngster!
This fun packed book teaches your child safety rules as he plays. For free copy, send to BMC Manufacturing Corp., Dept. S, Binghamton, N.Y.

Canadian Representative
STANDARD CYCLE PRODUCTS, LTD.
600 Victoria Park Ave. Toronto, Canada

KIDS! Here's the official Bike & Motor Club badge at your BMC Dealer

**Packard Roadster-Electric
Gendron
Opening Driver Door
tilt steering wheel
a very rare car - even
rarer with electric motor**

**U.S. Army Airplane
37" wingspan**

**Auto Racer
wood & sheet metal
leather seat
gas tank behind seat
rubber tired wire wheels**

NOEL BARRETT'S ANTIQUES & AUCTION

NEW HOPE, PA

Pioneer
sheet metal
metal wire wheels
decorated seat hinged
to reveal compartment

Henley Rollabout Scooter
wood & metal
original red & green paint

Keystone
wood & sheet metal
rubber tired wire wheels
cast iron crank

Stop & Go,
traffic signal for pedal cars
sheet metal

NOEL BARRETT'S ANTIQUES & AUCTION

NEW HOPE, PA

**Murray Racer with Windshield
delux model with horn**

**Caterpillar Tractor
electrically operated
moving treads**

**Sherwood Roadster-Futuristic
sheet metal three wheeler**

**BMC Special Racer
sheet metal**

1925 ALEMITE PAIGE

Gordon Clark, 3 years Old
Dec. 25, 1925

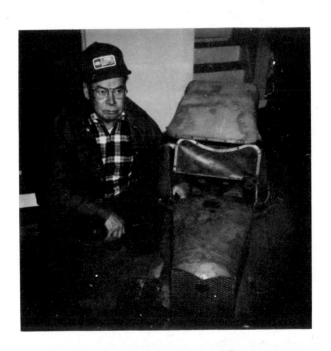

Gordon Clark When He Sold Car
Dec. 29, 1989

**Fred J. Brown 2 years old
Noel A. Brown 3 years old
From the State of Maine**

**Photo sent by Ed Weirick
Ellsworth, ME**

1928 American National - 1938 Picture
Bill Schroeder - Paducah, KY

1948 Murray Comet - 1949 Picture
Mark Morton - Riverside, CA

1926 Steelcraft - 1945 Picture
Larry Hathaway - Hiawatha, KS

75

**1941 Chrysler - 1934 Mack
Both Steelcraft**

**Danny & David Richter
Mentor, OH**

**1934 Mack
Steelcraft**

**William Reese
Greenlawn, NY**

**1916 Maker Unknown
1924 Picture**

**Evo Orsi
Chicago, IL**

1920s Maker Unknown

H. Fork
Gibsonburg, OH

1968 Murray Skipper

Owner & Driver
Dave Laduca
Lewiston, NY

1930s Maker Unknown
Driver Bill Giolma, 3 1/2 years old

Clive Giolma
Kamloops, Canada

1930s Maker Unknown
Driver Bill Giolma, 1 1/2

Clive Giolma
Kamloops, Canada

**1910s Pedal Car
Charles Squires
Mexico, MO**

**Photo furnished by
Portell Restorations
Hematite, MO**

**1920s Mack Steelcraft
Charles Squires
Mexico, MO**

**Photo furnished by
Portell Restorations
Hematite, MO**

**1920s Riding Horse
Unknown Source**

1960s Garton - 1963 Picture
Mark McDade - Hawthorne, NJ

1930 Garton
William Morgan
Garden City, MI

Original 1917 Calendar

A hundred per cent chauffeur in spite of his youth—only seven months old when this was taken

1910 Maker Unknown
Jack Pennington
Mocksville, NC

1910 Maker Unknown

1915 Irish Mail

Early 1900s

ACTUAL POSTCARDS

1937 Chrysler Airflow
Steelcraft

George Pancie
Olean, NY

1936 Skippy
1941 Picture

Gary Brady
Orange, CA

1934 Mack Steelcraft - 1948 Picture
David Richter - Mentor, OH

1918 Star Gendron - 1920s Picture
David Drane - Louisville, KY

81

DOWN MEMORY LANE

BOTTOM 5 PICTURES
BOUGHT AT ANTIQUE
SHOWS, ETC.

1925

1914

1921

1910

1920

1915

DRIVERS NOT IDENTIFIED

Ron Funkhouser
Tomsbrook, VA

**Ron Funkhouser & Daryl Funkhouser Sr.
In Their Pedal Cars in 1957**

**Misty Day Funkhouser 9 Months
Taken May 1980 In 37 Roadster**

**Daryl Funkhouser Jr. 3 Days Old
April 13, 1990**

**Daryl's Daughter Danielle
Taken In April 1990**

Funkhouser's Used Car Lot

Mid 1950s Side-Car Built & Restored by Ed Weirick – Ellsworth, ME
Morris Schalif – Roselle, NJ

YOU'VE GROWN MORE CONCERNED ABOUT AUTO SAFETY ...SO HAVE WE.

Driving was much simpler back then. But today, cars are faster and more powerful. Roads are more congested. And everyone talks about making driving safer.

The Hartford and AARP are doing something about it. That's why The Hartford Car Exhibit was designed.

This fascinating exhibit is filled with practical ideas for making driving safer and more comfortable. It helps *you* decide which safety features are best for you. Suggests ways to make you safer in your current car. And tells you some important safety advances to look for in a new car.

Through participative displays and video demonstrations, The Hartford Car Exhibit shows very clearly why air bags and antilock brakes are so important. How you can adjust seat belts for maximum safety. Even how you can check your reaction time.

This unique exhibit debuts at the June 1990 AARP Biennial Convention in Orlando, Florida. You can send for a free booklet capsulizing important safety tips from the exhibit.

To receive this booklet *free of charge*, or for information on the AARP Automobile Insurance Program from The Hartford—the only automobile insurance program designed especially for AARP members—write to: *AARP Automobile Insurance Program, Dept. DMS-127600, The Hartford Insurance Group, Hartford, CT 06155.*

AARP AUTOMOBILE INSURANCE PROGRAM
THE HARTFORD

It's time to get serious about auto safety.

Elmer Duellman and a part of his HUGE collection !!

If Elmer could count he would be surprised by the number !!

NOTES & INVENTORY

NOTES & INVENTORY

THE NEXT 10 PAGES
FURNISHED BY:

ELMER DUELLMAN
FOUNTAIN CITY, WI

Elmer is one of the largest collectors of Pedal Cars in the world. He also collects Antique & Classic cars. Without his help and encouragement this book or volume #1 could not have been completed.

ELMER, YOU ARE A GREAT GUY !

Thanks,

The Editor
Neil S. Wood

Elmer's First Pedal Car
1928 Steelcraft
He also has his first regular
car he bought - 1958 Chevy

1928 Packard
American National

1925 Packard
American National

1960s AMF
Amanda Duellman

1908 Boaz

1916 Garton

All Pedal Cars this page owned by Elmer Duellman, Fountain City, WI

**1920s Mack
Steelcraft**

**1930 Hudson
American National**

1922 Gendron

**1928 Packard
American National**

**Contemporary Poster
18" X 36"**

**Furnished by
Randall Arterburn
Indianapolis, IN**

**1936 Pontiac
Steelcraft**

All Pedal Cars this page owned by Elmer Duellman, Fountain City, WI

**1955 GMC Mail Truck
AMF**

**1950s Maker Unknown
Eric Duellman**

**Custom Made by
Tom Sturm
Riverside, CA**

1940 Triang

All Pedal Cars this page owned by Elmer Duellman, Fountain City, WI

**1925 Customized
One of a kind
Amanda Duellman**

**1955 Transport
AMF**

**1950s Fords
Maker Unknown**

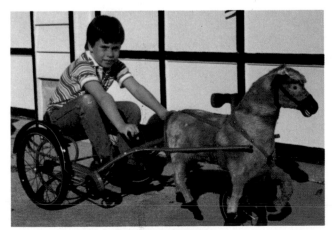

**1940s Sulky
Eric Duellman**

All Pedal Cars this page owned by Elmer Duellman, Fountain City, WI

1920s Steelcraft

1920s Garton

1941 Chryslers Steelcraft
Four of a Kind

1950s John Deere

1920s Toledo Wheel

1923 Cadillac 8
Gendron

1920s Gendron

1941 Steelcraft Buick

1933 Garton Buick

**1925 Hudson
Steelcraft**

1920s Garton

1947 BMC

**1908 Mascot
Maker Unknown**

1916 Gendron

1939 Skippy

1950s Allis Chalmers

1920s American National

1935 American National

1932 Gendron

1940s Garton

**1928 Jordan
American National**

**1955 GMC Tow Wrecker
GMC**

**1930 Mack Steelcraft
Custom one of a kind**

1930s American National

**1926 American National
Amanda Duellman**

Late 20s Hudson Racer

1921 Gendron

All Pedal Cars this page owned by Elmer Duellman, Fountain City, WI

1940s Austin Race Car

1940s Chrysler Stegar

1930s American National

1938 Skippy Lincoln

1930 American National

All Pedal Cars this page owned by Elmer Duellman, Fountain City, WI

1928 Fire Truck Cadillac - Eric
1930 Hose Truck - Amanda
Both American National

1950s Massey Harris

1955 GMC Fire Truck
AMF

**Thunderbolt
Maker Unknown**

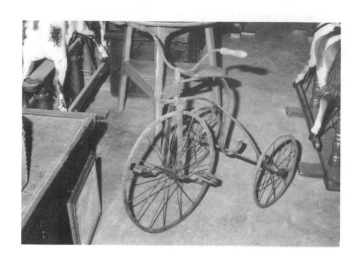

**Steel Wheel Tricycle
Maker Unknown**

**Hand Car
Maker Unknown**

**Pedal Wagon, 12 inch
Restored by Jim Geary
His Granddaughter & Friend**

**1937 Studebaker Riding Truck
Marx
Driver Niece Christina High**

**1937 Studebaker Riding Truck
Marx**

Photos by Jim Geary

Bull Dozer - Road Roller Riding Toy
Maker Unknown
Owner, Sandy Geary

1986 Reproduction
Studebaker Jr. Goat Wagon
Built by Jim Geary

1930s Studebaker Jr. Goat Wagon
South Bend Toy Co.

1930s Studebaker Jr. Goat Wagon
South Bend Toy Co.

1960 Larkette, Child's Gasoline Car
68", Master Enterprises

Many of the cars on this page
and the previous page were
restored by Jim Geary of
Goldsboro, NC

Doc Hunkler's Used Car Lot
Russiaville, IN

Toy Show Set Up
Very Nice

Robert Lampman
Vernon, NY

1906 Ford Custom

Elmer Duellman
Fountain City, WI

1940 Army Tank
Garton

Elmer Duellman
Fountain City, WI

102

1912 Ford
Maker Unknown

Elmer Duellman
Fountain City, WI

1952 Kiddillac
Garton

Paul Premer
Evans, CO

1934 Wagon

Paul Premer
Evans, CO

1930s Fire Truck
American National

Paul Premer
Evans, CO

1965 Indy Mustang
AMF

Tim Jones
Cincinnati, OH

1936 Ford Skippy

Tim Jones
Cincinnati, OH

1937 Ford Skippy

Tim Jones
Cincinnati, OH

Custom Low Rider

Tim Jones
Cincinnati, OH

1941 Chrysler
Steelcraft
Driver Lauren Singleton

Randall Arterburn
Indianapolis, IN

1926 Mack
Steelcraft
Driver Nick Singleton

Randall Arterburn
Indianapolis, IN

1924 Star
Restored

Tim Jones
Cincinnati, OH

1924 Pioneer

Tim Jones
Cincinnati, OH

**Allis Chalmers
1964**

**Mike Elwell
Cottage Grove, MN**

**Ford 8000
1968**

**Mike Elwell
Cottage Grove, MN**

**Murray P-610
1958**

**Mike Elwell
Cottage Grove, MN**

1962 Murray

Bob Ellsworth
Taylors, SC

Dump Truck
1950s Murray

Steve Powers
Moss Beach, CA

1950s Garton

Steve Powers
Moss Beach, CA

1940s
Maker Unknown
Driver Ricky Clemens Jr.

Rick Clemens
Beavercreek, OR

1960s Simflex

Joe Kirk
Shafter, CA

1960s Caterpillar
Driver, Ben Ragbuek

Chas Parker
Tarentum, PA

1960s AMF
Photo taken at National
Antique Advertising Show
Indianapolis, IN

1962 Flintstones
Irwin
Photo taken at National
Antique Advertising Show
Indianapolis, IN

1960s AMF
Photo taken at National
Antique Advertising Show
Indianapolis, IN

1950s Garton
Photo taken at National
Antique Advertising Show
Indianapolis, IN

1960s Murray
Photo taken at National
Antique Advertising Show
Indianapolis, IN

1970s AMF Fire Truck
Photo taken at National
Antique Advertising Show
Indianapolis, IN

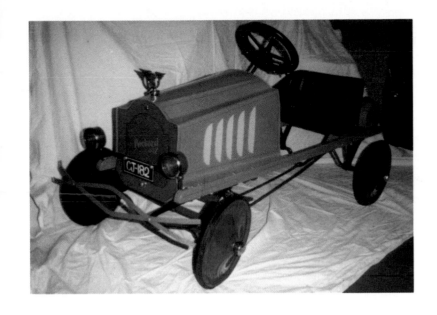

**Sidway - Topliff
1918 Packard Speedster**

**Bob Kellar
Sayville, NY**

**1937 Steelcraft
Airflow**

**Bob Kellar
Sayville, NY**

**1937 Steelcraft
Airflow, Restored**

**Bob Kellar
Sayville, NY**

"CREATION" Made from
Large Steelcraft Mack and
Old Steel Wagon

Bob Kellar
Sayville, NY

Pedal Car from Russia
Electric Lights, Coil Springs

Bob Kellar
Sayville, NY

1909 Early About

Ricker's Antiques
Mill Hall, PA

**1929 Cadillac
Boycraft**

**Kurt Hauschka
Rochester, NH**

**1947 Race Car
BMC**

**Ron Aust
Davenport, IA**

**1933 Chevrolet
Steelcraft**

**Calvin Chaussee
Colorado Springs, CA**

Old Pal

Abe Walp
Perrysburg, OH

Early 1920s Planes
Maker Unknown

Jack Williamson
Anderson, IN

1952 Murray Torpedo

Don Boring
Concord, TN

1960s AMF
Photo taken at National
Antique Advertising Show
Indianapolis, IN

1955 Murray
Photo taken at National
Antique Advertising Show
Indianapolis, IN

1955 Murray Dump Truck
Photo taken at National
Antique Advertising Show
Indianapolis, IN

1968 Murray Charger

Jim Wickfelder
Tinley Park, IL

1959 Garton "Auto" #5605
w/ Brittany Koch

Michael Koch
Thousand Oaks, CA

1958 Murray
Driver Brielle Marie Torel

Mr. & Mrs. M. J. Torel
Phoenix, AZ

1957 Murray

Joe Domanik
Racine, WI

1945 Murray

Joe Domanik
Racine, WI

**1950s Murray
1955 Chevy Custom**

Joe Domanik
Racine, WI

1935 Skippy Chrysler

Doc Hunkler
Russiaville, IN

1st on left
1935 Ford
American National

Doc Hunkler
Russiaville, IN

1932 Auburn
Steelcraft

Doc Hunkler
Russiaville, IN

Early 1900s
Maker Unknown

Steve Powers
Moss Beach, CA

1950s Garton

Steve Powers
Moss Beach, CA

1939 Lincoln
Steelcraft

Steve Powers
Moss Beach, CA

Garton

E. G. Cain
Westchester, OH

1962 Murray

Eric Woelbing
Franklin, WI

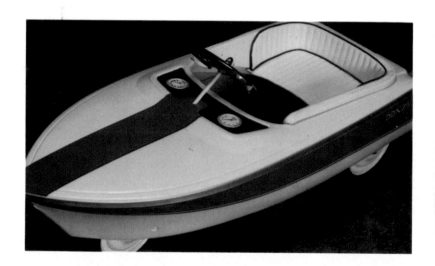

1960s AMF

Steve Powers
Moss Beach, CA

1960s
Maker Unknown

Don Woelbing
Franklin, WI

1928 Toledo
Hudson

Paul Premer
Evans, CO

Fire Chief Car
1961 Murray

Kasper
Waterford, WI

1961 Murray
w/U-Haul Trailer

Kasper
Waterford, WI

1941 Buick
Steelcraft

Randall Arterburn
Indianapolis, IN

1910 Pedal Wagon
Maker Unknown

Randall Arterburn
Indianapolis, IN

1955 GMC
AMF

Randall Arterburn
Indianapolis, IN

1934 Airflow
Garton

Randall Arterburn
Indianapolis, IN

1926 Star
Restored

Tim Jones
Cincinnati, OH

Dusenberg Race Car
1921 Replica

Pedal Car Classics
Fullerton, CA

1955 Murray
Driver D.J. Kasper

Kasper
Waterford, WI

1910
Maker Unknown

Richard Dodd
Springfield, MO

1932 Chrysler
Steelcraft

Richard Dodd
Springfield, MO

1935 Auburn

Richard Dodd
Springfield, MO

Garton
Late 50s

Donald Knox
Oshkosh, WI

American National
Early Teens

Elmer Duellman
Fountain City, WI

Austin
Mid 1930s

Gene Marschman
Clackamas, OR

1935 Austin
Made in England

Douglas Zingale
Minocqua, WI

1941 Chrysler
Steelcraft

Allen Wilson
Kingsville, TX

1926 Packard
American National

Allen Wilson
Kingsville, TX

Pedal Boats
1960s Murrays

John McKenzie
Seal Beach, CA

1941 Garton

Kasper
Waterford, WI

Model & Year Unknown

Kasper
Waterford, WI

1955 Murray

Kasper
Waterford, WI

127

1958 Murray Champoion

John Blanchard
Littleton, MA

1935 Essex
Steelcraft

John Blanchard
Littleton, MA

1948 Pontiac
Murray

E.G. Cain
Westchester, OH

1914 Pierce
Gendron

Dwight Sawyer
Chatham, NY

Graham - Skippy
1939

Richard Dodd
Springfield, MO

1925 Paige
American National

Earl R. Buske
Pocohontas, IA

1948 Firetruck Barber Chair
Murray

Bob Depenbrok
Arleta, CA

1914 Renault
Made in England

Ricky Clements
Beavercreek, OR

1935 Chrysler Airflow
Restored

Frank Gordon
Leawood, KS

1950s Jaguar XKE
Maker Unknown

Danny Fisher
Garland, TX

Steelcraft
Year ?

Kasper
Waterford, WI

1928 Packard

Kasper
Waterford, WI

1933 Steelcraft

Darwin (Doc) Hunkler
Russiaville, IN

1962 AMF

**Justin Schneider
Oak Creek, WI**

**1965 Mustang
AMF**

**Larry Schneider
Oak Creek, WI**

**1926 Restored
Gendron**

**Don Woelbing
Franklin, WI**

1948 Tow Truck
Murray

Todd Block
St. Peter, MN

1922 Oakland Uhlen
Driver Gene Kirsch's
Grandson Matty

Gene Kirsch
Roseville, MN

1933 American National
Driver Gene Kirsch's
Grandson Jimmy

Gene Kirsch
Roseville, MN

133

1949 Buick
Murray

Dwight Sawyer
Chatham, NY

1923 Steelcraft

Dwight Sawyer
Chatham, NY

1950s Ertel

Dwight Sawyer
Chatham, NY

**American National
1929 Restored**

**Richard Dodd
Springfield, MO**

**American National
1933**

**Richard Dodd
Springfield, MO**

**American National
1932**

**Earl R. Buske
Pocohontas, IA**

Left 1930s Steelcraft
Right 1960s Garton

E. G. Cain
Westchester, OH

1930s Steelcraft

E. G. Cain
Westchester, OH

Spirit of the 50s
E. G. Cain
Westchester, OH

**1937 Steelcraft
Fire Chief's Car**

**E. G. Cain
Westchester, OH**

**1956 Ford Station Wagon
Murray**

**E. G. Cain
Westchester, OH**

**1930s
Maker Unknown**

**E. G. Cain
Westchester, OH**

**Early Wagon
Police Patrol**

**Don Boring
Concord, TN**

**Left
Early Wagon**

**Don Boring
Concord, TN**

**Right
Early Wagon**

**Don Boring
Concord, TN**

Murray Champion
1950s

John McKenzie
Seal Beach, CA

Airplane
Early Teens

Joey Janots
Lodi, NJ

1950s AMF

Joey Janots
Lodi, NJ

**Station Wagon
1946 Murray**

**Photo taken
at Toy Show**

**Airplane
1945 Murray**

**Photo taken
at Toy Show**

**Woody Wagon
Garton, 1940**

**Photo taken
at Toy Show**

**1945 Murray
Pursuit Airplane
Steelcraft**

**Roy Juenemann
Wichita, KS**

**1936 Ford
Fenton**

**Roy Juenemann
Wichita, KS**

**1965 Mustang
AMF**

**Roy Juenemann
Wichita, KS**

**1918 Trimotor
American National**

**Kerry Holder
Springfield, MO**

1915 Chrysler

**Kerry Holder
Springfield, MO**

1930s AMF

**Charles Keehn
River Edge, NJ**

1989 'KING' Woodie Wagon
Suzanne & Emma Kenagy

Built by
Dick King
Kelso, WA

1989 "KING" Speedster

Built by
Dick King
Kelso, WA

1989 "KING" Fire Truck

Built by
Dick King
Kelso, WA

Maddie in her
first car

Phil Gottenberg
Galesburg, IL

Chevy, Year ?
Daughter Maddie

Phil Gottenberg
Galesburg, IL

Post War
Possibly English

Rex Barker
LaSalle, CO

1949 Murray Pontiac

Rex Barker
LaSalle, CO

1907 Pedal Train Engine
Maker Unknown

Rex Barker
LaSalle, CO

1989 "KING" Roadster

Built by
Dick King
Kelso, WA

1929 Model A Ford

Rex Barker
LaSalle, CO

Resembles 1953 Studebaker
Maker & Type Unknown

Rex Barker
LaSalle, CO

**Stearman Pedal Plane
Built 1989**

**Phil Gottenberg
Galesburg, IL**

**1930s Trike
Restored**

**Phil Gottenberg
Galesburg, IL**

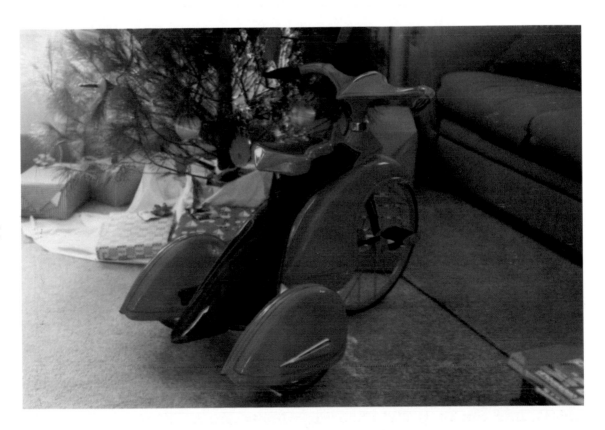

1926 "Allwin"
Richards, Son & Allwin
Birmingham, England
Operating Hood, Opening Door
Folding Windshield

Mike Hobday
Wales, UK

The car pictured above belongs to Ruth Memory which she received as a Christmas present in 1922. The little girls in the photo are her grandchildren, Katie and Beth Ann Memory.

The car is a Gendron "Stearns" with knuckle joint steering gear, flat wood steering wheel with gas control lever, horn, instrument board, motor meter, bumper, license tag, glass head lamps, hood vents, gear shift, gas tank, nickel plated hub caps, rubber decals, and ten inch plain bearing wheels equipped with half inch rubber tires.

Ruth P. Memory
Yucaipa, CA

148

1941 Chrysler
Restored

Phil Gottenberg
Galesburg, IL

Luke Smith test flying
Murray Patrol Pedal Plane
Restored by Steve Cousins

Ann Purucker
Prairie Village, KS

Late 1890s Tricycle

Roy Juenemann
Wichita, KS

**Supersonic Jet
1960 Murray**

**Terry Aldrich
Santa Maria, CA**

**Ford Woody
1949 Garton**

**Terry Aldrich
Santa Maria, CA**

**1970 Ranch Trac
Model E517**

**Terry Aldrich
Santa Maria, CA**

1920 Spirit of St. Louis
American National

Gene Burt
Pleasantville, PA

1928 Maxwell
Steelcraft

Photo taken at
Antique Show

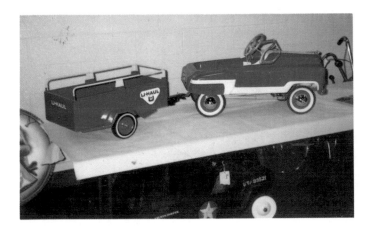

1955 Murray
W/ U Haul

Photo taken at
Antique Show

1926 Steelcraft Speedster

Don Boring
Concord, TN

1949 Garton
Station Wagon

Frank Speal's Auction
Hilliard, FL

1950s Wrecker
Hamilton

Blake Hughes
Kansas City, KS

Handbuilt 1925 American National Packard

Marc Olimpio
Wolfboro, NH

Roy Rogers "Nelly Belle"
All original, Late 40's - Early 50s

Art Stack
Buffalo, NY

Rather Unusual
Chain Drive, AMF
Late 60s - Early 70s

Art Stack
Buffalo, NY

**Murray T-Bird
Early 60s**

**Charles Branch
"Dr. J"
Marshall, TX**

**Steelcraft
1932 Packard**

**Paul Nestle
Nipomo, CA**

**1940s Mobo Pony Express
Home Restoration**

**William J. Torr
Northvale, NJ**

1969 Murray Camaro

**Steve Richter
Mentor, OH**

**Peerless Wolfpack
Made in Australia
1947-1950**

**David Barry
Epping, Australia**

1941 Chrysler
Restored

Frank & Irlene Gordon
Leawood, KS

1960 Kidillac
Restored

Frank & Irlene Gordon
Leawood, KS

1952 Murray Trac
Restored

Frank & Irlene Gordon
Leawood, KS

1924 Packard Six Roadster
American National

David Reed &
Blanche Gunther
Redding, CT

1921 Oldsmobile
American National

Ross Steele
Madisonville, IN

Fire Engine from ride
in Coney Island

Ray L. Albert
Dillsburg, PA

157

**Murray Dolphin
1960s**

**Don & Marge Wattawa
Milwaukee, WI**

**Chitty Chitty Bang Bang
1968**

**Stan Phillips
Oakmont, PA**

**Contemporary Restoration
1950s Jeep**

**Kurt Robidoux
Lincoln, NE**

**Brittany Koch riding
1983 AMF Fire Truck**

**Michael Koch
Thousand Oaks, CA**

**John Roy & Cinder with
1935 Skippy Fire Chief Car
Original Hat & Badge**

**Aaron Roy
Ashland, OH**

**Kevin Giolma riding
1962 Murray Station Wagon**

**Clive Giolma
Kamloops, B.C., Canada**

159

1961 Garton
Kidillac

Don & Marge Wattawa
Milwaukee, WI

BMC, Early 50s

Don & Marge Wattawa
Milwaukee, WI

1963 Garton Mark V

Don & Marge Wattawa
Milwaukee, WI

**1938 Garton
Lincoln Zephyr**

**Dennis Spadone
Denville, NJ**

**1949 Murray Torpedo
& Boat (rare with motor)**

**Dennis Spadone
Denville, NJ**

**Wesley Scott Wood
Editor's Grandson**

**Brand New
Caterpedal Bulldozer**

1903 MORS
Maker Unknown

Kerry Holder
Springfield, MO

Horse & Buggy
Maker Unknown

Kerry Holder
Springfield, MO

1918 Paige

Kerry Holder
Springfield, MO

Child's Pedal Car Restored
Early 1900
Seat can be raised or lowered

Robert Kyber
Chatham Township, NJ

Murray Super Sonic Jet
1952, Model K-900

John McKenzie
Seal Beach, CA

Same Jet
Before Restoration

163

1952 Murray
Fire Truck

Bob Ellsworth
Taylors, SC

AMF Taxi
60s - 80s

Bob Ellsworth
Taylors, SC

1951 Murray
Comet

Bob Ellsworth
Taylors, SC

Duesenburg
Boatail Racer
American National

Rex Barker
LaSalle, CO

"AMF" 1970s

Bob Ellsworth
Taylors, SC

1952 Murray
Dump Truck

Bob Ellsworth
Taylors, SC

1967 Murray

Bob Ellsworth
Taylors, SC

BEFORE

AFTER

1960S Murray
Restored
Speedway Pace Car

166

1924 Studebaker
Owner Max Corkins

Murray, Year ?
Driver Christina High

1951 Studebaker
Moskvitch Toy Co., Russia
Owner, Henry Muller
Child at car, Penny Muller

1951 Studebaker
Giordani Toy Co., Italy
Owner, Rex Barrett

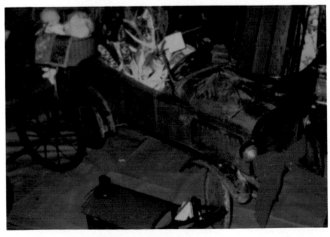

1930 Studebaker
Maker Unknown

Early Car
Maker Unknown

Photos by Jim Geary
Goldsboro, NC

1925 ALEMITE PAIGE
AMERICAN NATIONAL

This car was given away at a drawing on Dec. 25, 1925 at a 5 & 10 store owned by a German lady named Krotinger in a small town in northern Ohio. The lucky little boy was 3 years old. The boy and his dad went two miles into town on Christmas Eve 1925 and the boy's name was entered in the drawing. He was notified on Christmas day at 9 AM that he had won the car. He played with the car for about four years, then his mom put it the attic. The car remained there until Dec. 29, 1989 and was sold the next day. So he owned the car until he was 67 years old.

This car is the only one known to exist !

**Owned by Randall Arterburn
Indianapolis, IN**

**Chain Drive
Irish Mail**

Pedal Tricycle

**Pedal Horse Sulky
With Spoke Sheels
Stuffed Horse**

**Pedal Horse
Spoke Wheels**

Pedal Chariot

Italian Vespa
With Side Car
One of a Kind

Ed Weirick
Ellsworth, ME

Pedal Motorcycle by Mobo
Made in England

Ed Weirick
Ellsworth, ME

1937 Garton Trike

Ed Weirick
Ellsworth, ME

Mr. & Mrs. Harold Hemmelman
Centerville, WI
These Folks Are Great People.
They Also Restore Cars For
Elmer Duellman.

Mid 1950s Mercury
Restored by Ed Weirick
Ellsworth, ME

Owner - John White, Rams Head

1959 Mercury Promo
Fiberglass Body

Ed Weirick
Ellsworth, ME

Approx. 1910
Was electric, now gas
Driver John Buchanan

John Buchanan
Marine City, MI

1967 Mustang Jr.
12V Battery power
Driven by Katie & John Buchanan

John Buchanan
Marine City, MI

Cast Iron Horse Tricycle
Original Paint (8 colors)

John Buchanan
Marine City, MI

1957 Plymouth

Elmer Duellman
Fountain City, WI

1983 Roadmaster

Christa Coppock Driver
Gas City, IN

1920s Franklin
Mike Storhoff Driver

Restored by
Dan Storhoff
Dodge, WI

Motorcycle Bike
Irwin 1960s

Hidden Treasure Antiques
Franklin, OH

Early 1900s Go-Cart
Wicker Fold Up

L-B Antiques
Cedarville, OH

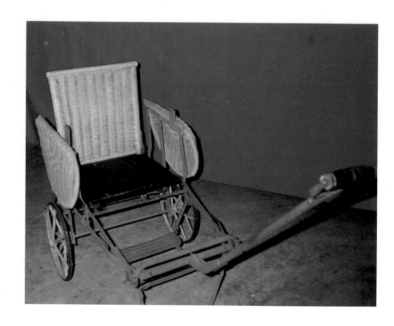

Mickey Mouse Wagon
Sibly Toy Co.

Roy Coulter
Dayton, OH

Grant Wood, 5 months
Editor's Grandson
Calling for Backup !

1928 Stearns Knight
Eric Duellman Driver
Fountain City, WI

1926 Jordan
Amanda Duellman Driver
Fountain City, WI

1952 Murray

**Bob Ellsworth
Taylors, SC**

1962 AMF

**Bob Ellsworth
Taylors, SC**

1960s Murray

**Bob Ellsworth
Taylors, SC**

Master Paul E. Bowman - Age 4, 1905
Maker Unknown

Same Car Today in Living Room of Owner
Blaine Linkous - Fallston, MD

Price Guide

The price guide in this book is for Pedal Cars in good to excellent condition. Cars found with parts missing, very poor paint, wheels changed from originals, or excessive rust will bring much lower prices. A car considered to be in good condition is one with original paint and no parts missing. A car in excellent condition is one that is 70% to 95% mint. This price guide is based on cars in these conditions. L-W BOOKS can not be responsible for gains or losses as this is only a guide.

PAGE 1
Top - $1500 +
Bottom - $1800 +

PAGE 2
Top - $300 +
Bottom - $150 +

PAGE 3
Top - $1900 +
Bottom - $2000 +

PAGE 4
Top - $1700 +
Bottom - $1700 +

PAGE 5
Top - $600 +
Bottom - $600 +

PAGE 6
Top - $200 +
Bottom - $300 +

PAGE 7
Top - $600 +
Bottom - $600 +

PAGE 8
Top - $600 +
Bottom - $100 +

PAGE 9
Top - $600 +
Bottom - $600 +

PAGE 10
No. 6400 - $125 +
No. 56 - $400 +
No. 47 - $150 +
No. 6100 - $100 +
No. 6800 - $125 +
No. 273 - $300 +
No. 60 - $100 +
No. 46 - $100 +

PAGE 11
No. 79 - $300 +
No. 55 - $200 +
No. 928 - $300 +
No. 49 - $300 +
No. 38 - $300 +
No. 936 - $400 +

PAGE 12
Top Left - $450 +
Top Right - $500 +
Bottom Left - $300 +
Bottom Right - $400 +

PAGE 13
Top Left - $175 +
Top Right - $300 +
Bottom Left - $300 +
Bottom Right - $700 +

PAGE 14
Top Left - $50 +
Top Right - $75 +
Middle Left - $75 +
Middle Right - $75 +
Bottom Left - $600 +
Bottom Right - $400 +

PAGE 15
Top Left - $800 +
Top Right - $600 +
Bottom Left - $600 +
Bottom Right - $800 +

PAGE 16
Top Left - $600 +
Top Right - $500 +
2nd Row Left - $600 +
2nd Row Right - $500 +
3rd Row Left - $900 +
3rd Row Right - $300 +
Bottom Left - $900 +
Bottom Right - $350 +

PAGE 17
Top Left - $400 +
Top Right - $300 +
Middle Left - $450 +
Middle Right - $30 +
Bottom Left - $450 +
Bottom Right - $450 +

PAGE 18
Top Left - $200 +
Top Right - $350 +
2nd Row Left - $200 +
2nd Row Right - $400 +
3rd Row Left - $700 +
3rd Row Right - $500 +
Bottom Left - $900 +
Bottom Right - $1000 +

PAGE 19
Top - $800 +
Middle - $900 +
Bottom Left - $600 +
Bottom Center - $700 +
Bottom Right - $400 +

PAGE 20
Scooter - $75+
Top Wagon - $100 +
Middle Wagon - $100 +
Bottom Wagon - $100 +
Top Car - $200 +
Bottom Car - $200 +

PAGE 21
Top - $200 +
2nd Row - $250 +
3rd Row Left - $30 +
3rd Row Right - $175 +
Bottom Left - $40 +
Bottom Right - $175 +

PAGE 23
R.A.F. Spitfire - $300 +

PAGE 24
U.S. Pursuit - $300 +

PAGE 25
Top - $200 +
Bottom - $200 +

PAGE 26
Top - $250 +
Bottom $450 +

PAGE 27
$650 +

PAGE 28
$650 +

PAGE 29
$600 +

PAGE 30
$500 +

PAGE 31
$350 +

PAGE 32
Top - $200 +
Bottom - $200 +

PAGE 33
Top - $100 +
Bottom - $100 +

PAGE 34
Top - $200 +
Bottom - $200 +

PAGE 35
Top - $500 +
Bottom - $500 +

PAGE 36
Top - $125 +
Bottom - $300 +

PAGE 37
Top - $300 +
Bottom - $300 +

PAGE 38
Top - $100 +
2nd Row - $100 +
3rd Row - $125 +
Bottom - $125 +

PAGE 39
Top - $100 +
2nd Row - $100 +
3rd Row - $125 +
Bottom - $100 +

PAGE 40
Top - $125 +
2nd Row - $125 +
3rd Row - $225 +
Bottom - $60 +

PAGE 41
BMC Car - $100 +

PAGE 42
Tractors $75 +
Blue Streak - $100 +
Thunderbolt - $100 +
Challenger - $100 +
Jet Liner - $100 +
Attachments - $25 +
Bicycle - $75 +
Wagon - $100 +
Racers - $250 +

PAGE 43
Reference Only

PAGE 44
Top - $75 +
2nd Row - $75 +
3rd Row - $100 +
4th Row - $100 +
Bottom Left - $50 +
Bottom Right - $200 +

PAGE 45
$175 +

179

PAGE 46
$100 +

PAGE 47
$200 +

PAGE 50
Top Left - $100 +
Top Right - $50 +
Middle Left - $100 +
Middle Right - $50 +
Bottom - $50 +

PAGE 51
Top - $75 +
Middle - $50 +
Bottom - $50 +

PAGE 52
Top - $50 +
Bottom - $50 +

PAGE 53
Top - $100 +
Middle Left - $75 +
Middle Right - $75 +
Bottom - $50 +

PAGE 54
Batman Plane - $20 +
Batman Copter - $20 +
Motorcycle - $200 +

PAGE 55
Top - $50 +
Middle - $50 +
Bottom - $50 +

PAGE 56
Top - $100 +
Bottom - $75 +

PAGE 57
Top - $50 +
Bottom - $75 +

PAGE 58
Top - $200 +
Bottom - $40 +

PAGE 59
Top - $50 +
2nd Row - $50 +
3rd Row - $50 +
4th Row - $50 +
Bottom - $50 +

PAGE 60
Top - $30 +
2nd Row - $200 +
3rd Row - $40 +
Bottom - $200 +

PAGE 61
Top Left - $200 +
Bottom Left - $30 +
Bottom Right - $100 +

PAGE 62
Top Left - $100 +
Top Right - $30 +
Bottom Left - $200 +
Bottom Right - $75 +

PAGE 63
Top - $150 +
Bottom - $150 +

PAGE 64
$175 +

PAGE 65
Top - $175 +
Bottom - $125 +

PAGE 66
Poster - $50 +

PAGE 67
Top Left - $2000 +
Bottom Right - $2000 +

PAGE 68
Top Left - $600 +
Top Right - $400 +
2nd Row - $800 +
3rd Row - $250 +
Bottom Left - $150 +
Bottom Right - $1500 +
Prices for Cars not Ads !
180

PAGE 69
Left - $150 +
Right - $100 +

PAGE 70
Actual Auction Prices
Top - $2600
Middle - $1000
Bottom - $1900

PAGE 71
Actual Auction Prices
Top Left - $2100
Top Right - $450
Bottom Left - $800
Bottom Right - $1250

PAGE 72
Actual Auction Prices
Top Left - $475
Top Right - $550
Middle - $250
Bottom - $230

PAGE 73
VERY RARE

PAGE 74
$200 +

PAGE 75
Top Left - $800 +
Top Right - $300 +
Bottom - $1200 +

PAGE 76
Top Left Car - $300 +
Top Right Car - $400 +
Middle - $600 +
Bottom - $400 +

PAGE 77
Top Left - $175 +
Top Right - $100 +
Bottom Left - $100 +
Bottom Right - $200 +

PAGE 78
Top - $600 +
Middle - $800 +
Bottom - $40 +

PAGE 79
Top Left - $200 +
Top Right - $800 +
Bottom Left - $75 +
Bottom Right - $500 +

PAGE 80
Top Left Card - $25
Top Left Car - $800 +
Top Right Card - $15
Top Right Car - $150 +
Bottom Card - $15
Bottom Car - $200 +

PAGE 81
Top - $800 +
Middle - $300 +
Bottom Left - $600 +
Bottom Right - $400 +

PAGE 82
Top Postcard - $15
Bottom 5 Pictures - $10
Top Car - $350 +
Middle Left - $800 +
Middle Center - $500 +
Middle Right - $400 +
Bottom Left - $300 +
Bottom Right - $500 +

PAGE 83
Top Left - $150 +
Top Right - $250 +
Middle Left - $200 +
Middle Right - $200 +

PAGE 84
One of A Kind

PAGE 85
Car - $1500 +

PAGE 90
Top Left - $1200 +
Top Right - $15,000 +
Middle Left - $150 +
Middle Right - $1500 +
Bottom Left - $300 +
Bottom Right - $700 +

PAGE 91
Top Left - $1200 +
Top Right - $2000 +
2nd Row - $600 +
3rd Row - $1800 +
Bottom - $400 +
Poster - $25

PAGE 92
Top Left - $400 +
Top Right - $400 +
Middle - $2000 +
Bottom - $400 +

PAGE 93
Top - $2000 +
Middle Left - $400 +
Middle Right - $200 +
Bottom - $250 +

PAGE 94
Top Left - $1500 +
Top Right - $800 +
Middle Left - Ea. $350 +
Middle Right - $300 +
Bottom Left - $1500 +
Bottom Center - $1800 +
Bottom Right - $600 +

PAGE 95
Top Left - $1000 +
Top Right - $1800 +
2nd Row Left - $1800 +
2nd Row Right - $800 +
3rd Row Left - $400 +
3rd Row Right - $900 +
Bottom Left - $400 +
Bottom Right - $800 +

PAGE 96
Top Left - $200 +
Top Right - $800 +
Middle Left - $1200 +
Middle Right - $900 +
Bottom Left - $200 +
Bottom Right - $1500 +

PAGE 97
Top Left - $400 +
Top Right - $2000 +
Middle Left - $1200 +
Middle Right - $1800 +
Bottom Left - $600 +
Bottom Right - $400 +

PAGE 98
Top - $800 +
Middle Left - $600 +
Middle Right - $1100 +
Bottom Left - $500 +
Bottom Right - $1400 +

PAGE 99
Top Left Car - $3000 +
Top Right Car - $2000 +
Middle - Ea. $200 +
Bottom - $400 +

PAGE 100
Top Left - $400 +
Top Right - $200 +
Middle Left - $175 +
Middle Right - $200 +
Bottom Left - $50 +
Bottom Right - $250 +

PAGE 101
Top Left - $200 +
Top Right - $800 +
Middle Left - $1600 +
Middle Right - $2000 +
Bottom - $600 +

PAGE 102
Middle Right - $1500 +
Bottom Left - $250 +
Bottom Right - $1500 +

PAGE 103
Top - $250 +
Middle - $150 +
Bottom - $800 +

PAGE 104
Top Left - $300 +
Top Right - $250 +
Bottom Left - $300 +
Bottom Right - $300 +

PAGE 105
Top Left - $300 +
Top Right - $2000 +
Bottom Left - $400 +
Bottom Right - $600 +

PAGE 106
Top - $75 +
Middle - $75 +
Bottom - $100 +

PAGE 107
Top - $150 +
Middle - $300 +
Bottom - $150 +

PAGE 108
Top - $250 +
Middle - $350 +
Bottom - $1000 +

PAGE 109
Top - $200 +
Middle - $500 +
Bottom - $200 +

PAGE 110
Top - $300 +
Middle - $75 +
Bottom - $100 +

PAGE 111
Top - $2000 +
Middle - $2000 +
Bottom - $2000 +

PAGE 112
Top - $2500 +
Middle - $300 +
Bottom - $800 +

PAGE 113
Top - $1800 +
Middle - $250 +
Bottom - $800 +

PAGE 114
Top - $150 +
Middle - Ea. $250 +
Bottom - $2500 +

PAGE 115
Top - $175 +
Middle - $250 +
Bottom - $600 +

PAGE 116
Top - $150 +
Middle - $250 +
Bottom - $200 +

PAGE 117
Top - $200 +
Middle - $750 +
Bottom - $800 +

PAGE 118
Top - $800 +
Middle - $900 +
Bottom - $900 +

PAGE 119
Top - $800 +
Middle - $200 +
Bottom - $300 +

PAGE 120
Top - $200 +
Middle - $100 +
Bottom Left - $100 +
Bottom Right - $200 +

PAGE 121
Top - $1800 +
Middle - $125 +
Bottom - $250 +

PAGE 122
Top Left - $400 +
Top Right - $1000 +
Bottom Left - $250 +
Bottom Right - $1800 +

PAGE 123
Top - $700 +
Middle - $475 +
Bottom - $150 +

PAGE 124
Top - $800 +
Middle - $2000 +
Bottom - $2500 +

PAGE 125
Top Left - $100 +
Top Right - $1200 +
Bottom Left - $300 +
Bottom Right - $300 +

PAGE 126
Top - $300 +
Middle - $2500 +
Bottom - $100 +

PAGE 127
Top - $1200 +
Middle -$150 +
Bottom - $250 +

PAGE 128
Top - $100 +
Middle - $600 +
Bottom - $200 +

PAGE 129
Top - $600 +
Middle - $400 +
Bottom - $2000 +

PAGE 130
Top Left - $1400 +
Top Right - $900 +
Bottom Left - $800 +
Bottom Right - $200 +

PAGE 131
Top - $200 +
Middle - $2000 +
Bottom - $1200 +

PAGE 132
Top - $100 +
Middle - $200 +
Bottom - $1200 +

PAGE 133
Top - $250 +
Middle - $800 +
Bottom - $900 +

PAGE 134
Top - $400 +
Middle - $700 +
Bottom - $100 +

PAGE 135
Top - $1200 +
Middle - $1800 +
Bottom - $900 +

PAGE 136
Top Left Car - $400 +
Top Right Car - $200 +
Middle - $400 +

PAGE 137
Top - $400 +
Middle - $125 +
Bottom - $800 +

PAGE 138
Top - $500 +
Middle - $500 +
Bottom - $750 +

PAGE 139
Top - $1000 +
Middle - $400 +
Bottom - $150 +

PAGE 140
Top - $300 +
Middle - $400 +
Bottom - $1200 +

PAGE 141
Top - $1000 +
Middle - $1200 +
Bottom - $300 +

PAGE 142
Top - $2000 +
Middle - $1200 +
Bottom - $600 +

PAGE 143
Top - $2000 +
Middle - $1000 +
Bottom - $3000 +

PAGE 144
Top - $900 +
Bottom - $800 +

PAGE 145
Top - $800 +
Middle - $600 +
Bottom - $2000 +

PAGE 146
Top - $1500 +
Middle - $900 +
Bottom - $500 +

PAGE 147
Top - $800 +
Bottom - $600 +

PAGE 148
Top - $3000 +
Bottom - $2500 +

PAGE 149
Top - $500 +
Middle - $1500 +
Bottom - $600 +

PAGE 150
Top - $300 +
Middle - $1200 +
Bottom - $200 +

PAGE 151
Top - $1000 +
Middle - $2000 +
Bottom - $500 +

PAGE 152
Top - Auction Price $7000+
Middle - $1200 +
Bottom - $300 +

PAGE 153
Top - $35,000 +
Middle - $1000 +
Bottom - $200 +

PAGE 154
Top - $200 +
Middle - $3000 +
Bottom - $200 +

PAGE 155
Top - $200 +
Bottom - $600 +

PAGE 156
Top - $500 +
Middle - $400 +
Bottom - $150 +

PAGE 157
Top - $6000 +
Middle - $2000 +
Bottom - $800 +

PAGE 158
Top - $350 +
Middle - $800 +
Bottom - $600 +

PAGE 159
Top - $100 +
Middle - $800 +
Bottom - $200 +

PAGE 160
Top - $500 +
Middle - $400 +
Bottom - $300 +

PAGE 161
Top - $1500 +
Middle - $1500 +
Bottom - $80 New

PAGE 162
Top - $2500 +
Bottom Left - $1500 +
Bottom Right - $600 +

PAGE 163
Top - $1500 +
Middle - $400 +

PAGE 164
Top - $400 +
Middle - $400 +
Bottom - $700 +

PAGE 165
Top - $1800 +
Middle - $300 +
Bottom - $700 +

PAGE 166
Top - $250 +
Middle - $75
Bottom - $400 +

PAGE 167
Top Left - $1200 +
Top Right - $250 +
Middle Left - $400 +
Middle Right - $600 +
Bottom Left - $1200 +
Bottom Right - $1500 +

PAGE 168
VERY RARE

PAGE 169
Top Left - $100 +
Top Right - $125 +
Middle - $200 +
Bottom Left - $200 +
Bottom Right - $200 +

PAGE 170
Top - One of a Kind
Middle - $400 +
Bottom - $75 +

PAGE 171
Bottom Left - $200 +
Bottom Right - $200 +

PAGE 172
Top - $1500 +
Middle - $300 +
Bottom - $800 +

PAGE173
Top - $500 +
Middle - $20 +
Bottom - $800 +

PAGE 174
Top - $100 +
Middle - $150 +
Bottom - $200 +

PAGE 175
Top - $60 New
Middle - $2000 +
Bottom - $2000 +

PAGE 176
Top - $250 +
Middle - $100 +
Bottom - $100 +

PAGE 177
Very Rare

PED'L POWER PRODUCTS ™

PRESENTS: "THE COLLECTABLES"
1st Edition — Color Art Lithograph Prints 16X20
Signed & Numbered 1—150 $125 each   P.P. USA